Health Goals and Health Indicators: Policy, Planning, and Evaluation

AAAS Selected Symposia Series

Published by Westview Press
1898 Flatiron Court, Boulder, Colorado

for the

American Association for the Advancement of Science
1776 Massachusetts Ave., N.W., Washington, D.C.

Health Goals and Health Indicators: Policy, Planning, and Evaluation

Edited by
Jack Elinson, Anne Mooney, and Athilia E. Siegmann

AAAS Selected Symposium 2

AAAS Selected Symposia Series

Copyright © 1977 by the American Association for the
Advancement of Science

Published in 1977 in the United States of America by

  Westview Press, Inc.
  1898 Flatiron Court
  Boulder, Colorado 80301
  Frederick A. Praeger, Publisher and Editorial Director

Library of Congress Cataloging in Publication Data
Main entry under title:
Health goals and health indicators.
   (AAAS selected symposium; 2)
   Papers presented at a symposium held at the 1977 AAAS
annual national meeting.
   Includes bibliographical references and index.
   1. Health planning--United States--Congresses. 2. Medical
policy--United States--Congresses. 3. Health status indi-
cators--Congresses. I. Elinson, Jack. II. Mooney, Anne.
III. Siegmann, Athilia E. IV. American Association for the
Advancement of Science. V. Series: American Association
for the Advancement of Science. AAAS selected symposium; 2.
RA395.A3H42   362.1'04'250973   77-14044
ISBN 0-89158-429-3

Printed and bound in the United States of America

About the Book

This volume brings together the perspectives and expertise of both medical and social sciences. The major topics include criteria for the determination of health goals, the analysis of health policies, and the indicators of health status that may be used to judge the consequences of health practices and policies.

Unmet health care needs, current national health policy and local planning, health data for policy and planning, and future directions in national health policy are also examined. These issues are then considered in light of the readiness of the sociomedical sciences to measure health status. Contributors discuss the behavioral measurement of health status, the measurement of psychological well-being, the assessment of dental health needs, and the possible impact of recently developed sociomedical health indicators on health policy.

Contents

Foreword

The *AAAS Selected Symposia Series* was begun in 1977 to
provide a means for more permanently recording and more
widely disseminating some of the valuable material which is
discussed at the AAAS Annual National Meetings. The volumes
in this *Series* are based on symposia held at the Meetings
which address topics of current and continuing significance,
both within and among the sciences, and in the areas in which
science and technology impact on public policy. The *Series*
format is designed to provide for rapid dissemination of information, so the papers are not typeset but are reproduced
directly from the camera copy submitted by the authors, without copy editing. The papers are reviewed and edited by
the symposia organizers who then become the editors of the
various volumes. Most papers published in this *Series* are
original contributions which have not been previously published, although in some cases additional papers from other
sources have been added by an editor to provide a more comprehensive view of a particular topic. Symposia may be reports of new research or reviews of established work, particularly work of an interdisciplinary nature, since the AAAS
Annual Meeting typically embraces the full range of the
sciences and their societal implications.

WILLIAM D. CAREY
Executive Officer
American Association for
the Advancement of Science

About the Editors

Jack Elinson, professor and head of the Department of Sociomedical Sciences at Columbia University, has coauthored two books, Public Image of Mental Health Services *(1967) and* Chronic Illness in a Rural Area *(Harvard University Press, 1959) and is coeditor of* Sociomedical Health Indicators *(Baywood, 1977).*

Anne Mooney, assistant professor in the College of Urban Affairs and Public Policy and the Department of Sociology at the University of Delaware, is the author of publications in the areas of health and social change, urbanization and human ecology.

Athilia E. Siegmann is a research assistant in the Division of Sociomedical Science at the Columbia University School of Public Health, concentrating on health economics and health status indicators. She is currently on assignment to the Bureau of Health Planning and Resources Development of HEW and is coeditor of Sociomedical Health Indicators.

About the Authors

Odin W. Anderson, professor of sociology and director of the Center for Health Administration Studies at the University of Chicago's Graduate School of Business, is the author or coauthor of five books on health care; most recently of **Two Decades of Health Services: Social Survey Trends in Use and Expenditures** *(Ballinger, 1976).*

Marilyn Bergner is associate professor in the Department of Health Services at the University of Washington and a consultant on the development and use of local health indicators. She is currently involved in research on health status indicators, including the Sickness Impact Profile.

Thomas W. Bice is a professor in the Department of Sociology at Washington University and specializes in health services research. He is a member of the Medical Sociology Section of the American Sociological Association Seminar Group on Health Status Indicators.

Norman M. Bradburn is the Tiffany and Margaret Blake Distinguished Service Professor and chairman of the Department of Behavioral Sciences at the University of Chicago. He is associated with the National Opinion Research Center and is the author of numerous books, reports and articles, including **The Structure of Psychological Well-Being** *(Aldine, 1970).*

Mary Jane Budenstein, a doctoral candidate in the Department of Sociology at Washington University, has collaborated in research on PSROs and Certificate of Need, and is currently concerned with decision theory as applied to prepaid group practice enrollment.

Harry P. Cain II is director of the Bureau of Health Planning and Resources Development at DHEW, and former director of DHEW's Office of Policy Development.

Willine Carr is a senior research associate at the Center for Health Care Research at Meharry Medical College and assistant professor in the Department of Family and Community Health at Meharry. She is coprincipal investigator of a DHEW-funded study on the effects of health care on outcomes.

Joel C. Kleinman, a service fellow at the National Center for Health Statistics, DHEW, has conducted research and written articles on methodological approaches to the use of data in health planning.

William B. Neser is a senior research associate at the Center for Health Care Research, Meharry Medical College, and associate professor and director of the Division of Graduate Studies in Community Health at Meharry. He is currently coinvestigator of a DHEW-funded study on the effects of health care on outcomes.

Mata K. Nikias, a senior research associate at the Center for Community Health Systems at Columbia University, has published studies of oral health status and is currently investigating patients' compliance in preventive dentistry regimens.

Lawrence T. Revo is a senior research associate in biostatistics at the Center for Health Care Research at Meharry Medical College and assistant professor of family and community health at Meharry.

Dorothy P. Rice is director of the National Center for Health Statistics at DHEW and is the author of many articles and reports on the financing of health care.

Helen N. Thornberry, associate director of Rhode Island Health Services Research, Inc., is currently on assignment to the Bureau of Health Planning and Resources Development at DHEW. She is the author of numerous papers on health information and planning, and data system development.

Samuel Wolfe, professor and head of the Division of Health Administration, Columbia University School of Public Health, has studied effects of various ambulatory care services on unmet needs levels in defined populations. He is the author of The Family Doctor *(Milbank, 1972) and coauthor of* Doctors' Strike *(Macmillan, 1967).*

Introduction

This volume considers the current status of health planning, health indicators that may be incorporated into the health planning effort, the current state of the art and future directions in the development of health status indicators, particularly sociomedical indicators, including indicators of mental health and of dental health.

For the first time in American history a federal law (the National Health Planning and Resources Development Act, P.L. 93-641) mandates that planners for the nation's health services must determine the health status of the populations served. Health planners and policy makers have special need for innovations in health status measurement. Some interesting and practical new developments in health status measurement for policy and planning are proposed by contributors to this volume.

Three out of four Americans see a doctor each year. There has been a four-fold increase in national health expenditures over the past fifteen years. The proportion of the gross national product spent on health care in 1980 is expected to be double what it was in 1950. How much evidence is there that all this medical care and expenditures therefor are effectively improving the health status of the American population? According to some critics, very little.

Is it because medical care has reached the limits of its effectiveness? Or is it because we do not have appropriate indicators of health status which can sensitively measure the real effects of medical care?

Using historical trends in mortality data some analysts conclude that medical care has indeed reached its limits of effectiveness or, as some argue, was never very effective relative to improvements in nutrition and in public and private hygiene. There is an alternative way of looking at the situation which may (or may not) yield a different

conclusion. That way is to develop and apply measures of
health status that more adequately reflect the intended impact of medical care. At the turn of the century people
died of diseases which today are preventable or curable.
Perhaps ten per cent of today's diseases are either preventable or curable with today's knowledge. Nevertheless, each
year 99 out of 100 people who are alive on January 1 are
alive on December 31. That's what mortality data tell us.
The relation between mortality data and the general health
of the population has yet to be determined. Today's
measures of health status should be sensitive to today's
ills. How then do we measure the health status of the
living?

     The alleviation of the impact of prevalent chronic
disease, the maximization of human functioning and the
improvement of a sense of well-being are appropriate goals
in modern society. We need ways of measuring the achievement
of these goals.

     The National Center for Health Statistics has an
extensive program of health statistics. Despite this program adequate health data for communities are lacking, as
Rice and Kleinman point out. "Existing general purpose data
systems were not designed to provide the kinds of data
essential for planning, managing, and evaluating programs at
State and local levels."[*] Perforce, synthetic estimates
based on national data are resorted to for communities.

     Cain and Thornberry raise the primary question as to
what should be realistic expectations for performance of
health planning programs. Do we have the knowledge to
evaluate the success of such programs? Once we do, they
note, we will be "...embarked on a regulatory road to
controlling activities in the health industry."

     After forty years of observation and careful study of
health systems in this and other countries, Odin Anderson
concludes there is only a "narrow range of policy options
that can be ideologically and politically entertained."
Aspirations should be reduced to attainable objectives.
Eschewing universal national health insurance he suggests
a readjustment of priorities which will deal more equitably
with the poor and powerless. The objective should remain
the cushioning of costs; it is wrong to rely on "our exceedingly crude health indicators."

---

[*]Health Statistics Plan, Fiscal Years 1978-1982. Department
of Health, Education, and Welfare. February 1977. Page 26.

That we may no longer need to rely on "exceedingly crude health indicators" is clear from Siegmann's review of research on health indicators over the past decade. Health status measures are now available which assess physical disability and social dysfunction and which are more reflective of chronic disorders and conditions characteristic of today's health problems. Siegmann distinguishes between "disciplinary" and "policy-oriented" indicators: disciplinary indicators describe the health status of the population much as light years measure the distance to the stars; whereas policy-oriented indicators, such as unmet needs for medical and dental care, point the way to social action.

An exemplar of disciplinary oriented indicators is the work of Bradburn on the measurement of psychological well-being. Bradburn asserts that for purposes of measurement it makes little difference whether one thinks one is studying mental health or illness or psychological well-being. A scale of psychological well-being is already being administered as a part of the National Center for Health Statistic's Health and Nutrition Examination Survey.

Measurement of unmet needs for health care is an example of policy-oriented assessment. Since the enactment of Medicare and Medicaid legislation more people have been receiving more medical care. Several papers in this volume, notably those by Wolfe et al. and by Nikias provide approaches to systematic quantitative methods for assessing unmet medical and dental needs in health service area populations. It is equitable to expect that whatever medical knowledge and technology can do should be generally available.

Bergner stresses that development of scaled indices of health-related dysfunction are especially pertinent for health planning and do not require that professionals assess the health of an individual. Sophisticated indices of health status have been formed based on information gathered by structured and standardized questionnaires. What is surprising to Bergner is that functionally based health status indices have not yet been considered by planning and policy makers to determine and support programs and policy decisions.

The "clamor about health care costs and reactive proposals to control them lose sight of the real...though... limited value of health care services." Bice and Budenstein insist therefore that health planning objectives require information on health status. Usable measures of health status should "attune policy makers and planners to

needs for and benefits of services as well as to their
costs."

Before concluding that medical care is exceptionally
wasteful or unnecessary, better evidence as to the impact of
medical care is needed. Whether medical care has an effect
on health status, or not, may be difficult to know until our
methods of assessing status are better. Likewise, unless we
monitor status, we will not be able to follow the effects of
our policies nor discover where inequalities in status
suggest deployment of additional resources. Containing
costs, however desirable, without consideration of the impact
of medical care on health status is just not enough by itself. Some new and practical ways to consider the impact
of medical care on the health status of populations are
proposed here.

                        Jack Elinson
                        Anne Mooney
                        Athilia E. Siegmann

Health Planning in
The United States:
Where We Stand Today

Harry P. Cain II and Helen N. Thornberry

Health Planning in the United States: Where We Stand Today

The purposes of this paper are to report on where we stand today (January 20, 1977) in the implementation of a national health planning program and to briefly discuss our most serious challenges and problems. As background, the history and highlights of the legislation under which the program operates are given.

The National Health Planning and Resources Development Act (Public Law 93-641) was passed in January 1975. After many months of hearings and debates, the Congress concluded that previous attempts to plan for health services and develop resources in a rational manner had not been successful, although there were some notable achievements within programs such as the Regional Medical Program, Hill-Burton and Comprehensive Health Planning, the progenitors of this legislation. The Congress found that there was an urgent need to restructure and strengthen areawide and State planning for health services, manpower and facilities. It was also evident that a national health planning policy which could provide guidance for the development of resources throughout the nation (especially medical facilities and new technology) and assistance in setting priorities for Federal programs and investments was required. In the absence of clear national goals and guidelines (and internally consistent Federal policies,) programs aimed at improving the system had been fragmented and uncoordinated---continuing or exacerbating existing problems of maldistribution and spiraling costs. As summarized in the Act, inadequate incentives to use appropriate levels of care and for the substitution of ambulatory, intermediate and home health care--- all less expensive than inpatient care---were found to have contributed to the cost spiral. The massive infusion of Federal funds in the 1960's into the existing system--with

no cost containment incentives, indeed with a number of cost
inflating pressures--contributed to the increases, and yet
failed to produce an adequate supply or distribution of
health resources for all parts of the country. Much of this
growth stemmed from the cost escalating character of the
system. For example, for institutions there is cost based,
retrospective, third-party reimbursement for services
rendered.

In general, it was evident in 1974 during the hearings,
that in some places in the nation, and for some services in
a number of locations, and for some sub-populations, there
were still serious problems of access to health care,
quality of care, and the availability of services, as well
as instances in which all citizens have not shared fully in
the benefits of social and medical progress in this century,
and in this legislation the Congress reaffirmed the nation's
commitment to quality health care as needed by all citizens.
However, it was manifest that the most serious problems con-
fronting the nation as a whole related to the burgeoning
costs of care and the seemingly endless possibilities for
care which stem from the technological and biomedical dis-
coveries in the past 10-20 years.

It is these latter two forces--cost increases and
technological advances--coupled with the changing age
distribution of the population and the growth in the number
of elderly with their higher service needs, and the shift
from the predominance of acute and infectious conditions to
chronic health problems---which have spotlighted a need for,
and triggered widespread interest in, improved health
planning and resources distribution in this nation. As the
total costs of health care and the proportion of the nation's
resources committed to health services expand there has
been, concomitantly, an emerging sensitivity to the finite-
ness of our resources.

Put another way, there is a new awareness that the
simpler questions about financing and planning for new
services and programs--the issues of the 50's and 60's--
which themselves have not been resolved completely--have
been replaced by the far more complex and threatening
questions concerning allocation of scarce resources in the
face of large and growing demands for services. To compli-
cate matters, health services, health, and quality of life
are all some of the most salient and emotional issues for
any nation or community. Further, in the health industry,
as the second largest employer of service workers (over
4.7 million persons) the issues related to jobs at a time of
high unemployment have surfaced as factors which cannot be

ignored. These issues can be especially critical at the
local level.

Recent figures on national health expenditures illustrate the seriousness of the cost problem. In 1960, the
total national investment in health care was 25 billion
dollars, $142 per capita, or 5.2% of the Gross National
Product. By 1970, the total investment had climbed to 69
billion dollars, or $334 per capita, (nearly twice as much),
and 7.2% of the GNP. For 1976, the total investment had
doubled again to 139 billion dollars and more than 8.5% of
the Gross National Product. Current projections for 1981
are for 264.3 billion dollars, $1159 per capita and a
startling 10.2% of the Gross National Product.

Presumably, the alarm with which these rapidly growing
investments are viewed would be tempered if they were clearly
purchasing improved health, more effective distribution of
diagnostic, curing and caring services, and eliminating
inequities in the system. Certainly some progress has been
made. For example, the traditional disparities in health
status and health services utilization by income and minority
group status have been narrowed, and for some conditions,
the death rates have declined.

However, the improvements in the system have apparently
been small, compared to the size of the increases in the
investment (1) and for some, such as the elderly, the actual
out of pocket expenditures over the same time periods have
increased, a problem for the elderly which was to have been
ameliorated by Medicare. Moreover, special programs such
as Medicaid, Maternal and Child Health, Women, Infant, and
Child Feeding and Nutrition, Community Mental Health Centers,
etc. have been seriously threatened by the government's inability to absorb the escalating costs of maintaining the
most essential (and legally required) programs. There is
also no way to know how many needed programs were never
initiated because established programs were struggling to
survive the budgeting process.

These higher costs have not only drained the public
purse, but in the private sector have been translated into
dramatic increases in the premiums paid for employees by
business, industry and labor. For example, the President
of General Motors reported that GM spent more for health
insurance coverage in 1975 than it did for steel---and that
is not meant to comment on the amount of steel in our cars!
Together, the big three automakers alone spent $1.04 billion
for health care benefits in 1975.

As an aside, related to the juxtaposition of automobiles and health care, we remember that it took the Arab oil boycott to demonstrate that the tragic toll in deaths and accidents on our highways could be dramatically reduced by a small reduction in the speed limit. In considering the future of health planning, the Congress was quite aware that if our interest is in improving health and in restraining the cost of medical care, we cannot concentrate all our attention on the medical care system alone.

Within this environment, the passage of Public Law 93-641 was intended to provide the structure and the support for effective health planning and a more systematic development of resources, especially new technology. A number of features were designed specifically to avert our drifting into a health care crisis of unsolvable proportions.

Public Law 93-641 added two amendments to the Public Health Service Act, Titles XV and XVI. Title XV requires the Secretary of Health, Education, and Welfare to issue guidelines, by regulation, concerning national health planning policy. The Guidelines must include:

1) Standards respecting the supply, distribution and organization of health resources.

2) And a statement of national health planning goals which must be expressed in quantitative terms, to the extent possible.

The Guidelines must be developed in consultation with a new National Council on Health Planning and Resources Development, Health Systems Agencies (HSAs), State Health Planning and Development Agencies (SHPDAs) and Statewide Health Coordinating Councils (SHCCs), which will be discussed later, as well as with organizations and associations representing the other provider and consumer groups. These guidelines will be more than national statements of values and preferences. Agencies must examine the relationship between the area's experiences and the national goals and standards and if the national priorities are not reflected in the area's goals, the agencies must explain the reasons therefor. Agencies will, of course, also deal with important local problems which are not addressed in the national guidelines.

Background work on the Guidelines has been underway for many months. In June 1975, a notice was published in the Federal Register inviting public comment and participation in the development of the guidelines, and draft materials have been circulated for public reaction. The draft guidelines include statements of general principles followed by specific goals and related sub-goals relating to health status, health promotion, health care and health financing.

There are also standards concerning the distribution and organization of health resources. For example, an upper limit on the number of beds per 1,000 persons and a minimum standard of physicians to population ratio have been suggested. A series of regional conferences on these guidelines is now being planned.

Title XV also mandated the creation of a National Council on Health Planning and Resources Development, composed of twelve public members, broadly representative of consumers, providers, health planning agencies and other qualified persons (2). The National Council is responsible for advising and making recommendations to the Secretary concerning the national guidelines, the implementation and administration of the program, and an evaluation of the implications of new medical technology for the organization, delivery and equitable distribution of health care services. To date, 5 (3) of the public members have been selected for the Council (and one preliminary meeting has been held).

To implement the law, the Congress authorized a network of areawide planning agencies, known as Health Systems Agencies (HSA's), which together will blanket the nation. Each agency is responsible for a health service area of approximately 500,000 to 3 million residents (4). The designated area is supposed to be a reasonable reflection of a health service or medical trade area with at least one center for the provision of highly specialized services. Wherever possible standard metropolitan statistical areas would fall into only one Health Service area. The provision resulted in 15 interstate HSA's.

The areas were selected by the Governors of each State under Federal guidelines (5). The designation of health service areas was completed early in 1975, though some modification of a few areas is still going on.

There are currently 212 health service areas. Of these, health service areas and State boundaries are coterminous in 10 locations. Under a special provision (section 1536) some States and territories were granted exemptions from the requirement to create a two-tiered (HSA and State) planning structure. The so-called 1536 entities include Rhode Island, the District of Columbia, Hawaii, the Trust Territories,

Guam, American Samoa and the Virgin Islands.

The Health Systems Agencies may be private nonprofit corporations, a public regional planning body if it meets special requirements, or a single unit of local government. Most of the designated HSAs are private nonprofit corporations (n=174; n=18; n=4 respectively). The agencies must be governed (6) by a majority (50-60%) of consumers, with the remainder of the Board representing physicians (particularly practicing ones) dentists, nurses and other health professions, health care institutions, insurers, professional schools and the allied health professions. The statute also requires representation of public officials, residents of non-metropolitan sub-areas, and HMOs, where appropriate.

An early study of governing boards of HSAs (based on 136 HSAs) revealed that consumers accounted for 52% (n= 3,105) of the 5,940 members surveyed. Another 2,078 were classified as direct providers (physicians, nurses, health care institution administrators, dentists, health and allied health professionals).

The purposes of the planning agencies are to

-- improve the health of residents of a health
   service area.

-- increase accessibility, acceptability, continuity
   and quality of health services provided.

-- restrain increases in the cost of providing
   health services.

-- and prevent unnecessary duplication of health
   resources.

The agency's primary responsibility is the provision of effective health planning for its area and the promotion of the development (within the area) of health services, manpower, and facilities which meet identified needs, reduce documented inefficiencies and implement the health plans of the agency.

The emphasis on improving the health of the residents is especially noteworthy and troublesome in light of the growing interest and in determining more precisely the relationships between health and medical services, and health and other non-medical factors and the difficulties associated with measuring such phenomena.

To meet these responsibilities, each agency must complete a Health Systems Plan (HSP) which is a statement of long range goals for the community. Not only are the Plans themselves considered important documents for the public statement of the community's goals and objectives, but the Plan serves as the basis on which all proposals for new institutional health services and programs, and applications for Federal funds under a significant number of Federal programs will be reviewed. In addition to the long range plan, there must be an Annual Implementation Plan which has specific objectives for each year or group of years within the minimum 5 year planning horizon of the HSP.

The agencies will also make recommendations to the State concerning projects for distribution of funds for modernization, construction and conversion of medical facilities, as well as review and make recommendations on proposals for new services and capital expenditures. Agencies will be reviewing existing services in terms of their appropriateness. In conducting these activities, agencies are required to coordinate with other Federally sponsored initiatives (e.g. PSROs and the Cooperative Health Statistics System), as well as existing planning activities under State and local agencies.

The Health Systems Plans for each area in the State serve as the basis for the State Health Plan.

The State Health Planning and Development Agency

To assure coordinated State level planning, an agency of State government, chosen by the Governor, is designated to serve as the State Health Planning and Development Agency (SHPDA). The SHPDA must have an administrative program approved by HEW for carrying out its functions.

The State Health Planning and Development Agency is responsible for conducting the State's health planning activities and implementing the parts of the State Health Plan and plans of Health Systems Agencies which relate to the government of the State. The agency will prepare a preliminary State plan from the Health Systems Plans for approval or disapproval by the Statewide Health Coordinating Council. The SHPDA prepares and assists the Council in the review of the State medical facilities plan and in the performance of its functions.

It serves as the designated planning agency under Section 1122 (capital expenditures review) of the Social Security Act if the State has made an agreement and admin-

istering a State certificate of need program of comparable
scope (7), reviews new institutional health services proposed and the appropriateness of existing institutional
health services.

The law also mandated the creation of Statewide Health
Coordinating Councils (SHCC) where the interests and perspectives of the HSAs and the State come together. Sixty
percent of its members are appointed by the Governor from
the State's Health Systems Agencies and have a consumer
majority. The Council reviews annually and coordinates the
Health Systems Plans and Annual Implementation Plans of the
State's Health Systems Agencies and makes comments to the
Secretary. The SHCC is responsible for the State Health
Plan (SHP) comprised of the Health Systems Plans. It also
reviews budgets and applications of Health Systems Agencies,
advises the State Agency on the performance of its functions,
and reviews and approves or disapproves State plans and
applications for formula grants to the State under a number
of Federal health programs.

   Certificate of Need. Of particular relevance to this
discussion is the law's mandate that all States develop a
Certificate of Need law which assures that only those services, facilities and organizations which are found to be
needed are offered and developed in the State (8). While
some States have had Certificate of Need laws since the
late 1960's, this is the first time that all States have
been required to institute such programs. Certificate of
Need (CON) attempts to prevent instances of blatant duplication of services and facilities which exist in some loca-
tions--e.g. hospitals within five minutes of each other
offering identical high technology services with neither
operating near capacity or even a minimum load for maintaining quality standards. Over the long run, CON attempts to
create a more coordinated, regionalized system for health
services.

The Certificate of Need laws will vary with each State,
within minimum Federal requirements, although all will include requirement for approval for any new construction or
significant capital expenditure (9). The Certificate of
Need section of the law augments the Capital Expenditure
Review provision (Section 1122) of P.L. 92-603, the 1972
amendment to the Social Security Act, which encouraged
States to participate in Capital Expenditures Review programs. In enacting the 1122 program, the Congress wanted
to make certain that reimbursement for depreciation under
Federal payments (Medicare, Medicaid, Maternal and Child

Health) was made in line with the then designated planning
agency's approvals. When all States have Certificate of
Need programs, which will have a similar, though generally
more comprehensive effect, there will be no further need
for the 1122 Capital Expenditures Review program.

The second major part of the Act, Title XVI, replaces
the older medical facilities construction program---best
known as Hill-Burton. The new program authorizes funds pre-
dominantly for modernization of medical facilities, construction of new outpatient or ambulatory facilities, and
conversion of existing medical facilities for the provision
of new health services. Money for construction of new inpatient medical facilities is available only in areas which
have experienced rapid recent population growth.

The implementation of Title XVI is also tied systemati-
cally to the entire health planning program, which was not
true in previous facilities oriented legislation. This not
only has the advantage of enhancing the rational development
of resources, but gives the planning side of the program
some further financial and political significance. For
example, the State Agency must have an approved State Medical Facilities Plan which is approved by the State Council
(SHCC), and is consistent with the State Health Plan (SHP).
While it is a separate document, the SMFP is considered to
be a more specific facilities-oriented part of the State's
plan for improved health. It is also the only plan to be
established under P.L. 93-641 which requires the approval
of the Secretary of the Department of Health, Education, and
Welfare.

The conceptually sound features have been, on the other
hand, an impediment to the distribution of the funds appropriated for the purposes of Title XVI. Until the planning
structure is in place, most of Title XVI cannot be implemented. The major exception is a project grant program
authorized by Section 1625 which provides some funds ($11
million dollars at present) for the modernization of public
medical facilities. Title XVI also authorizes an appropria-
tion for the HSAs to administer grants for planning and
development activities identified in the Health Systems
Plan. The Area Health Services Development Fund can be
used to stimulate the development of services but not for
actual delivery of services. As a whole, Title XVI clearly
indicates that the Congress was concerned with providing
resources to encourage the implementation of the Health
Systems Plans. P.L. 93-641 is not designed to create a
"paper planning process."

The total amount of money appropriated for all of the planning and regulatory activities was $128.59 million in FY 76, including 30 million for the transition from previous programs. (RMP, CHP, EHSDS). For FY 77, the actual amount of money available to support the HSAs and SHPDAs is increased, especially for the HSAs, although the total funds appropriated are smaller. The total FY 77 appropriation for planning is 125 million. The HSAs received a total of $64.09 million in '76 and will receive a total of $97 million for FY 77. However, the other parts of the program received either very small or no increases. For example, the technical assistance budget was reduced to $6.5 from $7.5 million.

While this sounds like a great deal of money, it is less than one-tenth of one percent of the total investment in health care for the same time period. Put another way, at the height of the appropriations envisioned for this program, we will be spending about 75¢/capita on health planning. That is hardly a major addition to the more than $600/capita this society is already spending on all our health activities. The relationship between the amount available for planning and regulation and the size and complexity of the system measured by its annual expenditures is important to bear in mind as a realistic assessment of potential of the program is made and as its effectiveness is judged in the coming years.

To summarize the status of this program, from another perspective, we already see the active involvement of more than 3,000 persons on the staffs of the planning agencies, 8,000 members of the governing boards, and many thousands more who are working on special study groups and task forces, all of them concerned with improving the health and health care in their communities. We do not have an energy problem in the health planning area.

What is different today. Since the nation has had some experience with planning, we are often asked what might make anyone feel that this program has any better chance of succeeding than the previous ones. Let us briefly note some differences in terms of (a) who cares, and why they care?, (b) the emphasis on plan implementation, through both positive action and negative sanction, (c) a more empirical, population-based approach, (d) the comprehensive scope and "systems" approach of the planning, and (e) the emphasis on technical assistance.

(a) Perhaps the most significant differences, comparing 1977 to 1966, are in the number and kinds of people who re-

cognize the problems and are willing to do something about
them. In the 50's the literature reflects an overriding concern for equity, access, poor health among minorities and
the low income citizens. In the 60's it was organization,
financing, improved productivity of particular services, and
a beginning of comments on costs. In the 1970's, there is
a predominant and widespread concern about cost increases
and the apparent endlessness of the spiral composed of increases in unit costs and increases in utilization, especially for diagnostic services, lab work and x-rays.

For example, the President of General Motors expressed
the industry's concern about the costs of health insurance
for employees and announced a commitment to changes to do
something about health care costs. As a result, the problems are much more visible and planners at State and local
levels are not struggling to influence the system in a
vacuum without support from business and industry. Governors, State and County legislators and administrators see
their annual budgets increasingly eaten up--and other programs cut--because of the rising costs of health programs.
They provide pressure for more direct action to contain unnecessary expenditures. In our program, this is exemplified
by insistent demands of the National Governor's Conference,
National Association of Regional Councils, and the National
Association of County Officials to help shape the design
and the administration of the planning program.

The rise in insurance premiums and demands for more
wages and other fringe benefits have become serious "trade
off" problems for labor unions. Larger unions which have
extensive health programs face the realities of rising
costs directly. As a consequence, there are new forces at
work in the planning arena. Labor and consumer groups are
willing to learn about the intricacies of the problems and
willing to stand with policy and decision-makers who have
to make and enforce some very difficult decisions.

(b) The second major difference is that the planning
agencies have some "teeth" in the legislation which most of
them did not have before, including Certificate of Need,
Capital Expenditures Review and review and approval of
public health funds in the area, and, in the future, review
of appropriateness of services (10). The addition of some
targeted stimulus money, through the Area Health Services
Development Fund (AHSDF), adds to the emphasis on plan implementation that was previously lacking.

(c) A third significant change in this program is the
importance given to the acquisition and use of empirical

data and a greater recognition of the value of an empirical
foundation for planning and evaluation. Planning agencies
are also being advised to develop a population-based approach to data acquisition, analysis and planning. That is,
we are encouraging the creation of the capability for examining statistics on utilization of services which can be
linked to a defined population (e.g. by using a geocode), as
well as data which may say something about people who do not
use the system. In addition, the development of the Health
Systems Plans for each area must involve the analysis of
health information and specification of goals and objectives
in quantitative terms, to the extent possible, with schedules for attainment of the objectives.

(d) The Plans must also describe and characterize the
status of the entire health system, noting the effects that
changes in one part of the system may have on other parts.
A comprehensive plan that must become increasingly specific
may not seem, on the surface, to be so different from some
done under CHP; however, the emphasis on a systemwide approach with specified, quantified goals, and the addition
of information on costs and financing (and the effects of
proposed goals on cost containment goals) are notably
different from most of the planning efforts under previous
legislation.

For example, the importance of viewing health as a
function of a number of factors is being reiterated. While
health planning has a variable ability to influence any one
of the factors, and planning agencies are specifically required to concentrate on planning for health services, the
agency must consider the array of influences on health. In
developing their plans, and in building the appropriate information resources, agencies are expected to identify all
relevant health factors and problems (11)--whether related
to life styles, human biology, environment, or the health
care delivery system (12), and, where possible, isolate
those conditions which can be addressed by the delivery
system. Included in the latter are health promotion programs which might be offered by health facilities which
encourage self-care and individual responsibility for eliminating self-imposed dangers to health. While there is an
emphasis on planning for health services, the agencies also
have an obligation to increase the visibility of other
factors and advocate, where appropriate, actions which would
improve the health of the people (13).

(e) The fifth major difference in this legislation is
the requirement that DHEW institute an intensive technical
assistance program. The program is spearheaded by ten

Centers for Health Planning--one in each DHEW region, initially funded for 2 years. The Centers provide training and on-site consultation to the agencies and serve as a focal point for an array of technical assistance activities such as short term statistical training, given under an agreement with the National Center for Health Statistics. The Centers also participate in the production of monographs and guidebooks by reviewing them for technical merit, utility, and relevance to the agencies' needs.

A National Health Planning Information Center, authorized in the law, has been opened since early 1975 as a clearinghouse for documents concerned with health planning methods, information methods for planning, health services research, and other research from related fields. NHPIC commissions the development of monographs and papers on specific topics for which there is a clear and immediate need, but no existing documents to fill that gap and serves as the publishing and dissemination arm for the Bureau.

To assist the agencies in meeting the requirements of the Act which involve the use of a great deal of health information, an agreement with the National Center for Health Statistics assures that there will be an acceleration in the implementation of the Cooperative Health Statistics System, a revitalized commitment to increasing the use of national data systems for local and State planning through research in small area estimating techniques, and a renewed effort to make data available to the agencies from existing systems.

Mrs. Dorothy Rice, Director, National Center for Health Statistics, has provided an enormous amount of support to this important activity and will be discussing some of their programs.

In short, a concentrated campaign for increasing knowledge about the state of the art and practice in health planning and related fields has been underway since the Act was passed. As a consequence, agencies will have far more data and knowledge of improved quantitative methods than before.

Some Persistent Policy Problems

Though we are encouraged by many aspects of this program and the way that it is developing, there are some persistent unresolved policy issues which involve the basic character or nature of what we are trying to do and which will benefit from more public consideration. Let us list at

least eight of what seem to be the most central of those
policy questions and then elaborate somewhat on each one:

1. What are the expectations regarding the performance
of the health planning program, and on what grounds can we
evaluate its success?

2. Do we have an adequate knowledge base on which to
build an effective, rational planning technology?

3. Are we going to allow the health planning agencies
to achieve some institutional maturity or is the health
policy environment in such flux that there are still several
changes ahead?

4. Can health planning be effectively disciplined and
resource conserving without any ceilings on total expenditures for health services and resources?

5. Can tough, negative decisions made by health planning agencies survive without a significantly raised level
of public awareness of the dynamics of the health industry?

6. Are the current mechanisms for assuring the public
accountability of health systems agencies adequate? What is
to be the long-run relationship between these quasi-public
agencies and our other more established approaches to conducting the public's business?

7. "Can the ranchers and the farmers be friends?" Can
the sometimes quite divergent interests of the consumers and
the providers of health care be welded in a health planning
agency to reach some reasonable common goals?

8. We are obviously embarked on the regulatory road to
controlling activities in the health industry; but whither
does that road lead?

You will accurately surmise from the substance of those
questions that we do not know the answers. We are fairly
confident, however, that these are among the more critical
policy questions for this country to answer if the health
planning program is going to serve us all well.

The first question, relating to expectations and future
evaluations should highlight the frame of reference with
which one approaches this program. We are confident that,
given the characteristics that distinguish this program from
those that preceded it, this program will do well -- compared
to the performance of those earlier programs (14). However,

the Congress was rather explicit in describing the grounds
on which this program is to be evaluated. Each year we are
charged with determining the answers to three simple questions in evaluating planning agencies' performance: (1)
has the health of the people improved?, (2) has the health
care system improved?, and (3) has the rise in health care
expenditures been restrained?

Obviously those three questions give us a couple of
problems. First, we do not know how to answer them; and
second, if we did, we suspect that the answer would not be
terribly encouraging. Over time, we can legitimately expect these planning agencies to help improve the health
care system -- but over how much time, and how we measure
that are still unknowns. The other two criteria for success
are obviously significantly more difficult to handle.

On the other hand, we may do well in establishing an
effective structure for allowing all concerned citizens to
become well informed on, and to play an active role in,
shaping the health care systems for their own communities.
We expect the long-run payoff from this program to be substantial along several dimensions, but do not expect it to
be all things to all people -- which a reading of P.L. 93-
641 might suggest the Congress had in mind.

On the "planning technology" question, the most urgent
need is for the development of improved methods for determining what medical technology, procedures, and therapies
are effective and needed, and under what circumstances. We
need to know what volumes of services are desirable for a
defined population, and what the optimal circumstances are
for assuring high quality care without unnecessary expenditures. For example, there are instances of very high priced
technology, which appear to have an open-ended potential for
use but a more limited potential for patient benefit, such
as CAT scanners, or coronary bypass surgery (15).

There is even some evidence that risks to the patient
for some procedures are substantial, especially when they
are done in locations which do not have sufficient volume to
maintain highly skilled and highly experienced teams (16).

We need standards and criteria for various types of
services, procedures and therapies within any one HSA.
Consumers and some Board members are at a serious disadvant-
age, in the absence of widely accepted standards and criteria, in reviewing requests from respected medical specialists for some new program or piece of equipment, even though

there may be substantial disagreements about effectiveness
and efficiency within the medical community. And across
HSAs, without such standards and criteria, we run the risk
of, unwittingly, exacerbating the maldistribution of resources. The three largest and oldest Federal programs
which are most involved in related research and could provide some relief to planners - NIH, NCHSR and FDA - form a
triangle which covers many very important research questions.
Unfortunately, in the middle of that triangle there is still
a large gap of knowledge and this is where the planners are
(17).

On the third question, pertaining to institutional
maturity, it is clear that to establish any effective new
institutional capacity to pursue the objectives of P.L.
93-641 will take several years of concentrated effort.
Buidling new institutions takes time; attracting adequate
numbers of talented people -- both volunteer board members
and professional staff -- takes the prospect of institutional stability.

As Professor Klarman has recently suggested, these
Health Systems Agencies must develop a posture of competence, fairness, impartiality, and an effective institutional memory, if they are to succeed (18). The question
is, will the Federal government provide the necessary continuity, length and strength of support to allow for that
necessary institutional development (19)?

The fourth question, relating to the need for a ceiling
on expenditures, under which planning should take place, is
a most pressing one. Given the way financial decisions are
reached in this industry, and the channels through which
money flows, it is very difficult for any Health Systems
Agency to determine what the cost of care is within its
area. Moreover, our third-party approach to payment for
health care ensures that when a Health Systems Agency makes
a poor decision, it will not have to pay the cost of that
decision, except in some unknown part. The cost of bad
decisions is borne by a great many insurance premium
holders, taxpayers and employers located beyond the boundaries of the health service area in question. That dynamic
has led a number of people to conclude that until we can
establish some effective ceilings on health expenditures,
health planning (concerned as it must be with issues of
access and quality as well as cost) will not develop the
discipline needed to conserve and properly distribute our
resources. Right now there is growing consideration in
Washington around the idea of establishing ceilings on
capital investments in health care, and some longer term

prospects of ceilings on operating expenditures as well.
We ourselves have some opportunities to move in this direction both through the National Guidelines required under
Section 1501 and through the criteria for the State Medical
Facilities Plan which we will have to issue soon. Under
those auspices we can develop approaches to putting ceilings
on the appropriate supply of facilities, and, to a lesser
extent, manpower resources by geographic area. Determining
how to do that wisely is one of our major challenges.

The fifth question pertains to another potential barrier to the success of the planning agencies -- the current
level of public understanding of the economic and health
problems which health planning agencies must confront. An
earlier paper set out this problem in the following, still
applicable manner:

Recognizing that in most areas of the health care
system we do not have criteria and standards on which to
base resource allocation decisions; and that when we do have
them, they will be less than totally objective and scientific; most of the agencies' plans, projects and decisions
will be judgment calls. Given resources that are not in-
finitely expandable, and the very sensitive objective of
enhancing our health and health care, the planning agencies
will often get into some very uncomfortable situations.
Moreover, since the agencies' decision-making processes will
be entirely open to public scrutiny and participation, most
everyone who cares will know what the agencies are doing.
The question is, will the concerned publics know what the
agencies are trying to do, will they understand the rationale, and will they support the outcome?

In the past several months, in various places around
the country -- including places having rather long histories
of health planning and certificate of need programs -- we
have seen county councils, State legislatures and Governors
(sometimes even Congressmen) overturn, or at least publicly
criticize and seek to overturn, decisions made by local and
State planning and regulatory agencies. And, there's a
certain pattern to those cases, a pattern in which the
planning agency has decided not to allow the building of
more of some aspect of the community's health care capacity,
to which the publicly elected officials have arisen in wrath
to denounce the heartlessness of the planners.

In general terms, we understand why that happens -- and
that it will continue to happen unless there is a significant increase in the public's awareness of how the health
industry works, what it costs, what it can and cannot do,

and who really pays the bills. The problem is that those
very important questions and issues are not simple. The
subjects are complex, confusing, and to most people who
have to worry about a lot of other things, they are not
even very interesting. Frankly, we don't know how to effectively raise the public's awareness of what's going on, but
we do know it must be done. It seems clear, at least to us,
that this impressive and peculiarly American effort to bring
rationality, wide accessibility and reasonable cost to our
health care enterprise, will not succeed unless and until
the public's general awareness of these subjects grows more
concerned and informed (20).

        Turning next to the questions of governance and ac-
countablity, the following major point should be made. As
the health planning agencies grow more effective, and have
more impact on the actual allocation of resources, the more
important will become the questions of the appropriate
auspices and governance of these agencies. Most of the
agencies are private non-profit corporations, accountable
to the Federal government and, in various, less direct ways,
to State and local governments and to the general public.
As they come more to "govern" developments in the health
sector, and as they conduct their business openly, they will
certainly become quasi-public institutions -- and be subject
to mounting pressure to be more directly accountable to the
publics for which they plan. P.L. 93-641 takes several approaches to assuring the public accountability of the health
systems agencies, but, the questions remain: a) will those
approaches (which are, in effect, guarantees of an open
process, with Federal and State reviews of performance) suffice over the long run?, and b) what effect will such quasi-
public structures have on the surrounding governmental
structures with which they will become so intertwined?
Professor Ted Marmor captured the essence of this question
in a recent observation; "the health systems agencies may
have more effect on the health of the polity than on the
health of the people" (21)!

        The next question relates to whether or not "the
ranchers and the farmers" can be friends. One of the fundamental assumptions on which this entire program is based is
that a community of interest, a set of shared perspectives,
can be developed between consumers and providers, insurance
carriers and policy holders, employers and employees, town
and gown, in the health sector. Out of those shared perspectives, it is assumed, Health Systems Plans -- and
regulatory decisions -- can emerge which "assure access to
adequate, appropriate health care at reasonable cost." To

develop such shared perspectives, all interests are to be represented on the planning agency boards -- a majority of consumers to be sure, but an effective minority of providers as well. That, it seems to us, is a promising and realizable prospect, and we are committed to working toward its reality.

There are, however, at least two other perspectives on this matter; they fall at opposite ends of P.L. 93-641. One of those perspectives, epitomized by Ralph Nader's Health Research Group (headed by Sidney Wolfe, M.D.), is that the clash of interests among the ranchers and the farmers is both inevitable and unresolvable except by regulatory fiat. According to this perspective, the inherently adversarial process forces the planning agencies to become regulatory bodies; and since their targets of regulation are the providers -- the physicians, hospitals, insurance carriers, etc. -- providers have no place on the boards of the agencies (22).

On the other side, there are frequently expressed provider viewpoints which are similarly contentious, holding that only providers should guide the development of our health systems. The common analogy is that of our only entrusting the flying of airplanes to highly trained pilots (23). The public policy question, of course, is whether we will side with any one religion and promote adversarial combat, or rather try to remain ecumenical, cosmopolitan, all-inclusive. (I'm sure our prejudice shows on this one.)

The final question and not unrelated to the previous one, pertains to the regulatory road down which this Law takes us. It has long been argued in various places that the competitive, economic marketplace dynamics do not work in the health sector. The reasons usually given pertain to the lack of cost consciousness on the part of either the consumer or the provider, the monopolistic characteristics of the profession of medicine, the ignorance of the consumer on medical matters, the "technological imperative". and so forth. The general conclusion from those arguments has been that the absence of market controls is so pervasive that the only hope is to have more regulation (24). Certainly the Planning Law is grounded in that school of thought. While implementing this law, we acknowledge the apparent lack of success of some regulatory efforts in other sectors of this society, but we are pursuing regulation in the health sector because a) we have no real alternative for both bringing these costs under control and at the same time assuring access to adequate care, and b) unlike other sectors' regulatory efforts, we intend to emphasize community-based planning -- planning <u>done</u> by all the key concerns in every community, and planning <u>upon which</u> reasonable regulatory decisions can be made. Further, we are trying to learn from studies of the weaknesses of other regulatory programs.

Though that line of reasoning is rather persuasive, there still remain some disquieting questions. For example, we know that there is disenchantment in this country with the capacities of large bureaucracies to competently respond to the interests they were designed to serve (<u>25</u>). And certainly we can anticipate the growth of ever larger bureaucracies concomitant with the stronger regulatory programs in the health sector.

That prospect is enough to make us nervous and to at least give a thoughtful hearing to those who are arguing that we are on the wrong road altogether. Certainly economists Martin Feldstein (<u>26</u>) and Alain Entoven (<u>27</u>), lawyer Clark Havighurst (<u>28</u>), Charles Schultze (<u>29</u>), and recently The President's Council on Wage and Price Stability (<u>30</u>) contend that we must make the market mechanisms work in this industry and that we should shy away from efforts to regulate in the place of an effective competitive enterprise. Those critics have a number of proposals worth consideration, certainly among the more academically inclined. We might note, however, the most of the "market place" proposals seem to us to hinge upon increasing the cost consciousness of both the individual consumer and the individual provider -- and we do not see any evidence of a societal interest in, for example, prohibiting first dollar coverage in the case of an expanded national health insurance program (<u>31</u>). Moreover, some studies have indicated that even when a health insurance program increases the cost sharing responsibility on the part of the consumer, that change may have only a short-lived impact on consumer behavior in health care.

While we, in the bureaucracy, recognize these issues, we do not spend a great deal of time debating them. Our first responsibility is to administer the law with as much sensitivity to the will of the Congress and to the interests of the public as possible. Not only does that turn out to be a full time challenge, but we also believe that there is ample opportunity within this legislation to find an effective balance between these two schools of thought and we are committed to making those ideas work. Perhaps in a few years we will know a little more about the potential for this uniquely American combination of forces and interests for planning for health, and modifications can be

made on the basis of knowledge and experience, not untested
speculation.

Given the size of the problems, the comparatively
limited funds available to support the program in such complex, controversial areas, and the absence of sensitive,
consistently reliable quantitative planning methods, it is
clear that the next few years will be challenging ones for
the planning agencies. In spite of all the issues we have
just mentioned, it is equally clear that planning in some
form or another is here to stay. This particular permuta-
tion has the characteristics of any program built upon demo-
cratic principles, with multiple layers of decision-making,
authority and responsibility.

It depends on being able to forge consensus, and on
being able to maintain enough consensus to support the very
tough decisions that are not far ahead. Decisions have to
be made and upheld by people and groups who have disparate
values, perspectives, preferences, and beliefs----some of
which are virtually sacred and all of which are salient.
The law creates and sustains an arena for resolving some of
these differences within the overall framework of community
goal setting and goal implementation. If all goes well,
this will result in fair, reasonable and cost constraining
decisions at local and State levels.

The question is not whether planning will survive but
whether or not this type of planning, with what some have
called its "town meeting" approach, will survive. Some
have said that this is the last chance for a program of its
type, with its emphasis on coordinating and catalyzing
voluntary involvement and private initiatives, to demonstrate its effectiveness. It is our feeling that this is,
in its broadest principles, the best approach for our
society, and that we must make it work. Approaches which
would involve less community participation can be avoided
only if we begin to make a demonstrable difference.

References

1. Also, questions have been raised about the negative effects of technology, especially when life has been prolonged at great expense and emotional burden to the family, even in terminal cases. This problem has created a debate which already involves complicated ethical, religious, legal and moral issues.

2. There are also 3 nonvoting ex-officio members including, the Chief Medical Director of the Veterans Administration, the Assistant Secretary for Health, Department of Health, Education, and Welfare, and Assistant Secretary for Health and Environment, Department of Defense.

3. Selection of all members has been delayed to assure proper consideration of candidates from a large number of planning agencies and the SHCCs.

4. There are particular exceptions for having a population less than or more than these preferences. For example, a SMSA with a population greater than 3 million may be a single HSA, such as New York City.

5. In only a few locations were the Governor's choices not accepted and then only when they were contrary to statutory requirements.

6. The Board can have no less than 10 or more than 30 members except where there is an executive committee composed of 25 members or less who can carry out most of the responsibilities of the entire Board. (see section 1512).

7. The law also provides minimum criteria for assuring that applicants for certification of need are guaranteed a fair and open review process, speedy consideration of their applications and appropriate channels for review and appeal.

8. As of today, there are only 2 States which have neither a Certificate of Need nor a Capital Expenditures Review Program in effect.

9. The minimum Federal thresholds for Certificate of Need reviews currently being proposed are:

   1) the offering or development of a new health care facility, or service by a health care facility or health maintenance organization.

2) a capital expenditure of $150,000 by a health
   care facility or HMO.

3) a change in bed complement.

10. While the only sanction related to appropriateness
    review is for the State Agency to make "public its
    findings", this can be a very influential factor in
    the ability to obtain support within a community.

11. In particular, agencies must assemble and analyze data
    concerning the health status of the population; the
    effects of the health system or health; the number,
    type and location of all health resources; the utili-
    zation patterns of services, the environmental and
    occupational safety factors which affect immediate and
    long term health conditions; the costs and financing
    of the health system.

12. M. LaLonde, A New Perspective on the Health of
    Canadians, Government of Canada, Ottawa, (April, 1974).

13. The problem of highway accidents is a good example of
    this issue. The solution to highway deaths lies not
    in medical care planning, although improved EMS can
    help to deal with the consequences of accidents.
    Agencies should also identify the problems and the
    relationships between health and accidents and advo-
    cate changes. As planning agencies, they also need to
    plan for improved emergency care.

14. There have been several evaluations of previous health
    planning experience. A good, recent summary is given
    by David Salkever, "Health Planning and Cost Contain-
    ment: A Selective Review of the Recent U.S. Experience,"
    International Conference on Programs for the Contain-
    ment of Health Care Costs and Expenditures. The
    Fogarty Center, National Institutes of Health,
    Bethesda, Maryland (June, 1976).

15. See both L. Thomas and R. Brook in Conference on Future
    Directions in Health Care: The Dimensions of Medicine,
    New York, New York (December 10-11, 1975), pp. 94-99;
    pp. 38-49.

16. Joint Commission of Accreditation of Hospitals,
    Accreditation Manual (1974).

17. K. White, M.D., "Ill Health and Its Amelioration:
    Individual and Collective Choices." Presented at the

Conference on Future Directions in Health Care (1976);
1977 The Dimensions of Medicine: New York, New York
(February 15, 1977).

18. H. Klarman, "Health Planning: Progress, Prospects and
     Issues." Paper prepared for University of Pennsylvania
     Bicentennial Conference on Health Policy, Philadelphia
     (November 11-12, 1976).

19. Salkever, Ibid.

20. Harry P. Cain, II. Presented at Region V meeting of
     HSAs and SHPDAs, Chicago, Illinois (September 27, 1976).

21. T. Marmor, Personal Communication. See also Harry P.
     Cain, II "Health Planning Program: Current Status and
     Issues," Annual Meeting of the American Association
     of Comprehensive Health Planning, Miami Beach, Florida
     (July 16, 1976).

22. T. Bogue and S. Wolfe, Trimming the Fat Off Health
     Care Costs: A Consumer's Guide to Taking Over Health
     Planning, Health Research Group, 2000 P Street, N.W.,
     Washington, D.C. 20036.

23. See, for example, Russell B. Roth, M.D., AMA News,
     (November 22, 1976) p. 2. Dr. Roth elaborates on the
     analogy by noting that "Passengers who insist on fly-
     ing the airplane are called hijackers." (p.11)

24. The traditional view is summarized in Victor Fuchs
     Who Shall Live, New York (Basic Books, Inc. p. 102-
     103. See also, among many possibilities, Economic
     Aspects of Health Care Ed. by John B. McKinlay,
     Milbank Memorial Fund, New York, 1973).

25. C.C. Havighurst, "Regulation of Health Facilities and
     Services by Certificate of Need," Virginia Law Review
     599 (October) 1143-1232.

26. M. S. Feldstein, The Rising Cost of Hospital Care,
     Information Resource Press, Washington, D.C. (1971).

27. A. C. Enthoven, "The Impact of Legislation on Capital
     Development for Health Facilities." Presented at the
     Conference on Capital Financing Alternatives for
     Health Facilities at the University of Pittsburgh
     (November 19-21, 1976).

28. Havighurst, Ibid.

29. C. Schultze, "The Public Use of Private Interest,"
     Harper's, Vol. 254 (May, 1977) pp. 43-62.

30. The Rapid Rise of Hospital Costs. Executive Office of
     the President's Council on Wage and Price Stability
     Staff Report (January, 1977).

31. Some of these thoughts stemmed from discussions with
     Herbert Klarman.

2

National Health Data for Policy and Planning

Dorothy P. Rice and Joel C. Kleinman

Few people now dispute the need for data as a basic requisite for the development of policy in every area of our
national life, whether it be health, defense, agriculture,
transportation, welfare or any other. We shall assume you
agree and take this opportunity to provide a few specific
examples of how data have been or could be used both in the
development of health policy at the national level and to
assist health planning at the local level. We will also indicate some of the problems, concerns, and obstacles we face
in the further development of health data for policy and
planning.

Organization of Federal Health Statistics

Before getting into specifics, it may be useful to out-
line the current scope of health statistics and the authori-
ties under which the National Center for Health Statistics
(NCHS) operates.

The history of Federal health statistical activities
goes back to the last century when information on births and
deaths was collected periodically by the Bureau of the
Census. In 1946, this function, by then based upon registra-
tion systems covering all States, was moved to the Public
Health Service. The National Health Survey Act of 1956 authorized a continuing survey and special studies of sickness
and disability in the United States population. Since those
days, the health statistical programs have continually adapted to better meet the emerging needs of an expanding community of data users. In 1974, P.L. 93-353 renewed the au-
thorities under which the NCHS had operated and in effect,
redesignated the NCHS as the focal agency for the collection
and analysis of a broad range of data on the health of the
Nation. More than twenty data systems are currently operating in the NCHS to produce information on health status of

the population, health resources, utilization of health services, nutrition and family growth as well as on the Nation's
patterns of births, deaths, marriages, and divorces.

Cooperative Health Statistics System

In addition, P.L. 93-353 granted authority and support
for Federal participation in an effort to build a health data
system which could serve as the basis for effective planning
at all levels and for all areas of the country. Although
developmental work on this system--the Cooperative Health
Statistics System--was authorized earlier, it was Public Law
93-353 of 1974 that authorized the Secretary of the Department of Health, Education, and Welfare, "to assist States in
the design and implementation of a cooperative system for
producing comparable and uniform health information and statistics at the Federal, State and local levels."

The Cooperative Health Statistics System is designed to
provide the framework for a coalition among the various
levels of government and the private sector for the production of health statistics. Input is obtained from data users
at the National, State and local levels regarding data they
need, turnaround time they require, and the desired frequency
and reliability. The agreed upon data items are collected by
the level best equipped to collect them and the data are then
shared with all users. NCHS has the responsibility for providing National leadership by coordinating efforts among
Federal agencies and between the Federal Government and the
States, and in assuring the quality and comparability of data
collected. The CHSS will help mold the current fragmented
data collection activities throughout the country into a co-
hesive system. This should result in savings in data collection costs, a greatly reduced burden on data providers, and
more important, data will be comparable and in the requisite
detail for most uses by all participants in the system.

In terms of actual implementation, all but five States
have implemented one or more of the seven data components of
the System. Each of these components has common core items
--that is, the minimum data set of information which is required at all levels. Of course, in many cases, States and
localities will need more information and greater detail
than are specified in these minimum sets of data. These
needs can be met by building additional items onto the core
and by conducting periodic and ad hoc surveys. The collection of the core information is being conducted under agreed-
upon standards, definitions, and procedures, and the data
thus gathered are to be shared with the other levels of

government and the private sector. In most instances, collection and processing occurs at the State level, and ele-
mentary units of data are being transmitted to the Federal
level under a cost-sharing arrangement. We are on our way to
a full, coordinated network in which statistical operations
at the State and local levels will be obtaining the data they
need about health status and problems in their own jurisdic-
tions, and will be providing the Federal government with minimum sets of data which are comparable among all reporting
areas.

Advisory Committees

P.L. 93-353 also authorized the United States National
Committee on Vital and Health Statistics (USNCVHS), first
established in 1948, which provides a communication link between the public and private sector. This Committee is the
primary outside advisory group on matters of health statistics to the Secretary and the Assistant Secretary for Health.
With staff support from the NCHS, the Committee stimulates
studies and provides advice on statistical approaches to
health problems of National or international interest, on
health statistics and health information systems, and on a
range of health statistical issues and activities that affect
health care policies.

A second committee, this one within the government, was
established in 1974. The Health Data Policy Committee advises the Assistant Secretary for Health on current and long-
term data needs for planning and management, on policies and
procedures for coordination of health statistics activities,
on proposals for major new health statistics systems, and on
uniform minimum basic data sets.

The Committee has developed into an effective vehicle
for a coordinated approach to data oriented health policy
issues. It provides an internal forum for discussing and
resolving specific issues and a focus within the Department
for liaison and cooperative arrangements with other agencies.
Active participation of representatives from the Office of
Management and Budget, the Department of Defense, and the
Veterans Administration provides the Department with valuable
information on the related experience and data requirements
outside of the Department.

Examples

With this background, we would like to turn now to four
specific examples of how Center data can be used in national
health policy and local health planning.

Unnecessary Utilization of Services

Cain and Thornberry emphasized that the rapid increase in medical care costs was the primary reason for current health planning efforts and, indeed, for the emphasis on a policy for cost containment in the health area. In Fiscal Year 1976, health expenditures reached $139 billion, a 14 percent increase over the 1975 figure. This represented 8.6 percent of the Gross National Product (GNP). How can national health data assist in designing strategies for reducing the rate of growth in expenditures? One possibility is in the identification of areas in which services may be over utilized, resulting in unnecessary expenditures. Surgical procedures provide some examples. In particular, a recent report (1) from the Professional Activity Study (PAS), a hospital discharge abstracting service, showed a sharp rise in hysterectomies based on reporting from their member hospitals (a 21 percent increase from 1970 to 1975).

The NCHS' Hospital Discharge Survey (HDS), a probability sample of short-stay hospitals, can be valuable in monitoring trends such as this. In fact, the HDS data also show the incidence of hysterectomies rising substantially. The rate per 100,000 females 15 years and older was 734 in 1971 compared to 850 in 1974, a 16 percent increase. This represents 125,000 additional hysterectomies per year and (based on the 9.5 average stay observed in 1973) 1.2 million hospital days. The total cost of these 125,000 hysterectomies is roughly $200 million (based on a surgical fee of $450 (2) and hospital expense per patient day of $119 (3)).

Furthermore, both PAS and HDS data show the increase varied substantially from one region of the United States to another. This variation is consistent with small-area variation observed in other studies (4, 5). The large increases in hysterectomies and their variability by geographic region suggests that this is an area in which the indications for surgery are not well-defined. This suggestion is supported by a recent study based on a program which required second opinions by consultants prior to surgery (6). In that study, one-third of the recommended hysterectomies were not confirmed. Thus, the cost-saving potential in this area is obviously great. Other surgery for which we are seeing increases include Cesarian section (44 percent increase between 1971 and 1974), vascular and cardiac surgery (36 percent increase), and orthopedic surgery (28 percent increase).

Of course, these data raise a number of questions which require further study. What was the reason for the increase? Why did it vary by region? Does the regional variation in

the incidence of hysterectomy relate to regional differences
in the incidence of diseases which are indications for
surgery or to regional differences in surgical practice?
Finally, before implementing policy to control unnecessary
surgery, even more difficult questions must be addressed:
what are the appropriate indications for the procedure?
Under what conditions will this procedure improve the individual's health? What are the potential risks? How do
alternative therapies compare in terms of risks and benefits?
These are the kinds of questions raised by Cain and
Thornberry for the scientific community.

Hypertension

Let us turn now to a different problem--a case for which
there is both an effective therapy and greater agreement that
the therapy is appropriate. The policy issues involve how to
make this therapy available to those who need it.

Hypertension has been clearly established as a precursor
of heart disease, stroke, and kidney disease. Since it often
presents no symptoms, hypertension may be present long enough
and at high enough levels to cause serious damage before the
individual is aware of it. Although the causes of most cases
remain unknown, drugs have been shown in clinical trials to
reduce hypertension and its ensuing consequences.

The seriousness of hypertension and the availability of
effective therapy have led to a number of Federally-aided
efforts to detect and control hypertension. Prevalence data
from NCHS were used in the original development of these
programs; recent estimates from two of our surveys can be of
further assistance in refining these efforts and in formula-
ting other policies in this area.

There are two major sources of data on hypertension
within NCHS. The first is the Health and Nutrition Examination Survey (HANES), which administers medical examinations
and questionnaires to a probability sample of the noninstitutionalized population. During the period 1971-1974, HANES
collected data about hypertension from over 13,000 persons
aged 18-74 years. The second data system is the Health
Interview Survey (HIS), which provides data based on household interviews, again of a probability sample of the non-
institutionalized population. Responses to a series of
questions about hypertension included in this survey in 1974
are available for 25,000 persons 17 years of age and over.
Based on HANES, the prevalence of hypertension (as defined
by systolic blood pressure above 160 mm Hg or diastolic
pressure above 95 mm Hg on the first reading) was 23.2

million adults or 18 percent of all persons 18-74 years of age (7). The prevalence rate among blacks was nearly twice as high as that among whites. There were 4.3 million additional persons who had normal or borderline blood pressure readings but were taking drugs for hypertension. Thus, hypertension represents a significant health problem in the United States.

Those responsible for screening programs to deal with this problem can use our data to select the target populations which will yield the greatest payoffs. The HANES data indicate that 63 percent of the males and 47 percent of the females who were identified as "definite hypertensive" had not previously been told they had hypertension. The proportions were highest among the younger age groups--nearly 70 percent of the men and 65 percent of the women aged 18-34 who were identified as definite hypertensive were unaware of their condition.

Data from HIS show the experience of those who do not report having hypertension in terms of whether their blood pressure had been tested within the past year. Among males 18-34, less than 60 percent had a blood pressure check within the past year, compared with 75 percent of the women. These findings suggest that the screening strategy for this age group should emphasize the need to identify male hypertensives, possibly through on-the-job screening programs.

Follow up of effective screening with effective therapy is, of course, crucial. Our data apply here as well. The HIS findings indicate that 75 percent of persons reporting that they had hypertension had medications prescribed. Of these, 25 percent are no longer taking medication. Furthermore, HANES data show that more than half the persons taking antihypertensive medication do not have their hypertension under control. We are now undertaking a more detailed analysis of the reasons people discontinue their drug therapy. Preliminary results show that lack of understanding of the importance of long-term regular therapy, inconvenience and costs of drug .therapy, and side effects all contribute to noncompliance. The detailed analyses point to specific aspects of .hypertension control upon which health education should concentrate. The great advantage of using NCHS data for these issues is that our data systems are population-based, avoiding the possibility of misleading biases which arise in retrospective studies of selected patient populations.

On a very pragmatic level, HANES data has proved useful in allocating funds for hypertension programs to the States.

The distribution of Federal funds to states for screening for and treatment of hypertension is required to be based in part on the prevalence of hypertension in each State. Although the HANES sample could not provide State estimates directly, it was possible to develop "synthetic" State estimates of prevalence. The basic idea behind such estimates is simple: prevalence of hypertension is known to vary by age, sex, and race (among other factors). HANES data can provide prevalence estimates for each age, sex, and race group based on national (or regional) data. Since the Census Bureau produces age, sex, and race distributions for each State, it is possible to multiply the HANES prevalence data by the State population in each age, sex, and race group, and add to obtain an overall estimate of hypertension prevalence for each State. While this method is subject to many difficulties, it does at least go one step beyond an assumption of constant prevalence in each State in the distribution of hypertension funds.

Medically Underserved Areas

My next example of the uses of NCHS data will illustrate two issues. First, it will show the difficulties in implementing Federal policies at the local level without local data. And, second, it will show how one national data system, the Health Interview Survey, can be used to provide guidelines for these policies by using the more complex statistical methods.

Our national concern for equal access to health care has been translated into a large number of Federal laws which give special emphasis to medically underserved or health manpower shortage areas. The most comprehensive attempt to go beyond health manpower to population ratios in identifying underserved areas is the Index of Medical Underservice (IMU) which is used to designate medically underserved areas (MUAs) under the HMO Act and other health service programs. The IMU is a composite of four variables (infant mortality rate, physician to population ratio, percent of population below poverty level, and percent of population over 65). These variables are weighted to predict the areas that a group of informed experts would judge as medically underserved.

The use of such indirect measures to designate MUA's is the result of a lack of uniform small-area indicators across the United States which are more directly related to access to medical care. Although the HIS collects a great deal of information on utilization of health resources and, in 1974, included a special supplement on medical care

needs, it can provide only national or regional estimates.
Thus, it is impossible to use HIS data directly to designate
MUAs.

It is possible, however, to use the HIS data to assist
in critically examining MUA designations. Such a study is
now in progress and the preliminary results for nonmetropolitan areas show that the differences between MUAs and non-
MUAs are not as great as might be expected. For example,
there was little difference between MUA and non-MUA respondents in the proportion with a usual source of care (80 percent in MUAs vs. 83 percent in non-MUAs). The proportions
with no physician visit within the past year were also similar (29 percent in MUAs vs. 27 percent in non-MUAs) and the
number of physician visits per person per year were identical (4.5).

It is possible to go even further and use the HIS data
together with Census data, vital statistics, and manpower
data, which are available for small areas, to define an index which is better able to discriminate between underserved
and non-underserved areas. By choosing a few key variables
which reflect access (e.g., availability of a usual source
of care, absence of problems which delayed or prevented
needed care, etc.), it is feasible to use multivariate statistical methods to choose those variables available at the
local level which best predict medical underservice.

Small-Area Data For Local Health Planning

The previous example illustrated the problems with using
HIS data at the local level. What types of data are then
available for the local Health Systems Agency (HSA) in meeting its mandate for health data at the local level? The Cooperative Health Statistics System (CHSS) discussed earlier
will certainly go a long way toward meeting the need for
local data. Until that system is fully implemented, however,
there are some limited data which can be very useful in local
health planning.

The National Health Planning and Resources Development
Act of 1974, P.L. 93-641, requires that local Health Systems
Agencies "assemble and analyze" a wide variety of data including those related to health status and the determinants
of health status. Yet, the measurement of health status is
still in its infancy. We are also quite far from being able,
even in a research context, to assess the effects of the
health system on health status, as HSAs are required to do.

How, then, can an HSA meet the requirements of the Act?
Although there are no data available at the local level to
measure meaningful overall health status indexes, it is
possible to address certain limited aspects of health status
with data from the vital statistics system. The mandate for
local health status data in P.L. 93-641 has generated renewed
interest in the development of innovative approaches to the
analysis of vital statistics and their application to health
planning.

The use of natality and infant mortality data in planning maternal and child health programs is one area in which
health status data is relevant to health planning. For example, despite the large decreases in infant mortality in
recent years, there remain very large geographic variations
in mortality during infancy. In fact, during the period
1974-1975, the infant mortality rate for certain medium-sized
nonmetropolitan counties was 19 percent higher for both white
and black infants than the corresponding rates for suburban
counties of large metropolitan areas. The white/black differences also remain large: in 1975 the black infant mortality rate was 85 percent higher than the white rate. The
black rate was fully 25 years behind the white rate. These
considerations have led to a new effort on the part of the
Bureau of Community Health Services to revitalize State
maternal and child health programs. The vital statistics
system allows the planner to examine county infant mortality
rates over long time periods (as published for example by
the Maternal and Child Health Studies Project (8)). Thus,
the planner can identify areas with consistently high rates
or unusual shifts in rates which indicate the need for appropriate intervention.

Natality data can also be useful to the planner for a
number of purposes. First, in 42 States, data on the birth
certificate indicate the month or trimester in which prenatal care began and the number of prenatal visits. These
data provide an indication of areas or population subgroups
(e.g., teenage mothers with no high school education) who are
not receiving adequate prenatal care. Furthermore, intervention to improve the level of prenatal care can be evaluated rather quickly and inexpensively by using birth certificate data. Although the evidence is not conclusive, there
are indications that adequate prenatal care is a determinant
of healthy newborns (9).

Another example of the use of natality data at the local
level is in planning and evaluating family planning programs.
A priority of family planning programs is the reduction of
birth rates among mothers at highest risk of infant loss

(e.g., teenagers, woman over 35 or 40, women with large numbers of children, etc.). The distribution of births by
these characteristics can be used in targeting programs to
meet the needs of high-risk women, and by following births
over a period of time, in evaluating the success of the programs. It is also relatively easy to "translate" the distribution of births into expected infant mortality rates which
can then be compared with actual rates.

Finally, the infant's birth weight (which is given on
the birth certificate) provides another health status measure which should be examined to identify those mothers at
risk of low birth weight infants.

Still another example of the uses of mortality data
which goes beyond the population of mothers and infants is
the examination of small area death rates for specific
causes. Dr. David Rutstein and his colleagues (10) have
listed causes of death which are preventable under current
medical knowledge. Thus, areas with high rates for these
causes could be examined to detect any deficiencies in their
health care delivery system. We are beginning to study geographic variations in these cause-specific death rates.

Of course, mortality does not provide a complete picture of health status. Some conditions which kill cause
relatively little disability before death while other conditions which seldom cause death (such as arthritis) are
responsible for a great deal of disability. However, given
the limited resources of the HSAs and the limited knowledge
about how to measure health status and its determinants,
focusing upon the indicators provided by vital statistics
seems a reasonable interim strategy.

CONCLUSIONS

We hope these examples give some flavor of the diversity of issues which can be addressed at both the national
and local levels by current health data. We are developing
a systematic approach to meeting the needs of policy-makers
at the Federal level. At the same time, we are cognizant of
the State and local needs and have begun to address them.
We are working closely with BHPRD in several areas.

First, in order to meet the challenges facing health
planners and policy-makers, a strong commitment to increased
training is required. Short-term training courses for planners have been developed by the Center's Applied Statistics
Training Institute (ASTI). ASTI now offers eleven courses
related to the use of data in health planning and evaluation.

Second, we are providing technical assistance in the
form of "Statistical Notes for Health Planners" that are
sent to the Health Systems Agencies. These notes are designed to help agencies fulfill the requirements of P.L.
93-641 relating to the assembly and analysis of data. The
notes provide the methodology for using existing data available from Federal programs, and occasionally include actual
data for illustration. For example, the note on infant mortality included infant mortality rates for each HSA.

We also prepared a publication of "Selected National
Data Sources for Health Planners" which serves as a directory
of Federal Statistics which are useful to planners.

Let us conclude by indicating a few specific areas which
we see as crucial in data collection and use for the development of health policy and planning.

First, we need more research on measurement of health
status, with particular emphasis on how health policy and
planning can have an impact on health status. The papers in
this volume represent an important contribution to research
in this area. However, we need to go still further to develop methods for including the more comprehensive health status
indicators on the Center's ongoing health surveys. Furthermore, we need to link health status measurement research to
health policy and planning efforts. P.L. 93-641 requires
that HSAs and the National Health Planning Council develop
goals which "to the maximum extent practicable, shall be expressed in quantitative terms." How can analysis of historical data best be used to develop realistic quantitative
goals? For example, the infant mortality rates for whites
and blacks have been decreasing at rather constant rates
(4 percent per year for whites and 3 percent per year for
blacks) since 1965. Should the goal for 1980 merely be an
extrapolation of that trend? Should we expect the trend to
level out? Or should we seek to accelerate the decrease?

Second, we need research on appropriate levels of
health resources and services. For example, as of
December 1973, there were 15 non-Federal physicians in
active practice for every 10,000 persons in the United
States. Yet, the variation among Health Service Areas was
from 4 to 44 physicians per 10,000, an eleven-fold difference. The difference in hospital beds per 10,000 was not
quite as large but still varied five-fold (from 16 to 84
beds per 10,000). What is the appropriate level? Which
characteristics of the population (e.g., age, sex, socio-
economic measures, health status measures) should be taken
into account in determining the optimal level? Once the

optimal level is determined, what strategies are effective in bringing an area up (or down) to this level?

Third, we need to further develop mechanisms for shared data systems as a method for reducing data collection costs and respondent burden. The Cooperative Health Statistics System discussed earlier is designed for this purpose. However, the full potential of the Cooperative System will be reached most quickly and efficiently by the development of strong, well-staffed State Centers for Health Statistics in each State. These centers would serve as focal points for the assembly and analysis of all health data and have responsibility for primary data collection and activities for at least one of the statistical components of the System. The centers should also have the capacity for analysis of health-related data, from whatever source, and be able to provide consultation to planning agencies and other users on the limitations and potentials of available data as well as on needs for additional information and how it can be secured. Several states now have such centers, and we are hopeful that others will follow their lead.

Finally, the commitment to increased training must be extended beyond specialized courses to health professionals. Undergraduate as well as graduate education should include more opportunity for critical, quantitative thinking about health issues. This is especially evident in the emphasis that P.L. 93-641 places on consumer participation in health planning.

On the other hand, graduate programs in statistics need to emphasize the uses of data to a much greater extent than is currently the case. All too often, graduates of such programs know little about the substantive issues on which the data are brought to bear.

The need is great for new interdisciplinary programs which will provide persons trained in the application of quantitative techniques (such as statistics, economics, epidemiology and operations research) to health policy and health planning. This may perhaps be done most effectively by post-doctoral training of social scientists, statisticians, epidemiologists and other health professionals in an environment which applies knowledge and techniques from these fields to health issues. It is only by removing these artificial disciplinary barriers that we will begin to develop really effective health planning.

References

1. B. W. Perry, PAS Reporter, 14:9, Aug. 23, 1976.

2. G. J. Schieber, et al., N. Engl. J. Med., 294, 1089, (1976).

3. American Hospital Association, Hospital Statistics, (Chicago, 1976).

4. J. Wennberg and A. Gittelsohn, Science, 182, 1102, (1973).

5. J. Wennberg and A. Gittelsohn, J. Maine Med. Assn., 66, 123 (1975)

6. E. G. McCarthy and G. W. Widmer, N. Engl. J. Med., 291, 1331 (1974).

7. J. Roberts and K. Maurer, Advance Data, No. 1, Department of Health, Education, and Welfare, PHS, HRA, National Center for Health Statistics, (1976).

8. M. W. Pratt, et al., Infant and Perinatal Mortality Mortality Rates by Age and Race, (Maternal and Child Health Studies Project, MSRI, Washington, D.C., 1976).

9. D. M. Kessner, et al., Infant Death: An Analysis of Maternal Risk and Health Care, (Institute of Medicine, Washington, D.C., 1973).

10. D. D. Rutstein, et al., N. Engl. J. Med., 294, 582, (1976).

3

Unmet Health Care Needs and Health Care Policy

Samuel Wolfe, Willine Carr,
William B. Neser and Lawrence T. Revo

I. INTRODUCTION

This paper on Unmet Health Care Needs and
Health Care Policy consists of three major parts:
First, the position will be advanced that unmet
health care needs can be measured. Second, the
extent to which such measurements can be linked
to the technical capability of the National
Center for Health Statistics, and to the evolving
role of the Health Systems Agencies under
PL 93 - 641, the National Health Planning and
Resources Development Act, will be explored.
Third, the extent to which such factual data can
lead to health policy based on priority setting,
assessment of needs, and cost containment, will be
discussed.

II. MEASUREMENT OF UNMET NEEDS FOR HEALTH CARE

In a recent monograph edited by Jack Elinson,
we discussed unmet needs indicators. (1) Unmet
needs indicators, as one type of sociomedical indicators, are being developed because of the
relative inadequacy of traditional morbidity,
mortality and other biomedical data to indicate
population health levels and effects of differing
kinds of health programs. (2)

In general unmet needs can be defined as the
differences in care for the appropriate treatment
of specific health problems and the care actually

The research being carried out by the Center for Health Care Research at Meharry Medical College, Nashville,
and referred to in this paper is supported by research grant HS-01710 from the National Center for
Health Services Research, HRA, PHS, DHEW.

received for these problems. Thus, unmet needs
look at "deficits" in care where care is required
and relate to society's capacity to care for the
sick.

Unmet needs can be measured using various
methods as described in the monograph edited by
Elinson. Population-based unmet needs assessments are based either on review of existing data,
or are based on newly gathered data obtained
through physical examinations and/or interview
surveys. Obviously the latter approaches are
more expensive than the former but may yield far
more specific and relevant data for health policy
makers, as detailed later in this paper.

One important recent example of an unmet
needs indicator derived from survey data is found
in the work of Taylor, Aday, and Andersen on the
development of a symptoms-response ratio. (3)
The symptoms-response ratio summarizes the difference between the reported number of visits
which survey participants made to a physician in
response to specific symptoms and the number of
visits which a panel of medical experts estimate
should occur for these same symptoms.

This method is simple and obviously far less
expensive than clinical examinations and may serve
as an indicator of equity of access for various
population sub-groups. But it is based on reports, it ignores asymptomatic problems (such as
breast lumps, high blood pressure, prostatic
cancers, and so on), and it relies on external
judges who make judgments that are not individua-
lized to the real life professionally - judged
needs of specific persons in specific situations.

An example of unmet needs assessments based
on clinical examinations, is our own research
currently under way at Meharry Medical College in
Nashville, Tennessee.

This is a two-part study which was begun in
1970 and is due to be completed in late 1977.
The Study of Unmet Needs is evaluating the relative success or failure of comprehensive care with
broad outreach, comprehensive care with limited
outreach, and traditional care in reducing levels

of unmet needs in defined populations over time.
We have defined unmet needs as the absence of any,
of sufficient, or of appropriate care and services
which are judged necessary to deal with defined
health problems. We view changes in unmet needs
as outcome measures which can be used to evaluate
the effectiveness of health services delivery
alternatives. (4)

Two primary methods of data collection are
being utilized. These methods include (a) household interviews to obtain information about the
family unit, and (b) detailed clinical evaluations
which provide information on selected individuals.
Household interviews are conducted at every sample
household. An average of one person per household
is then randomly selected to take part in a detailed health examination during which a physician, dentist and nurse examine and interview the
clinical evaluees. Selected persons are paid a
small amount of money to take part in these clinical evaluations. Following the examinations
the health professionals make judgments about
problems and unmet needs for care or services.
Also, during the household interview and clinical
evaluations, individuals are asked, to a limited
extent, to express their own judgments about
unmet needs.

Through the household interviews, neighborhood residents trained as interviewers obtain demographic data, on housing and neighborhood problems, information on employment, economic security and food costs, information about the health
of each family member, and a limited amount of
information on self-perceived needs.

As part of the detailed clinical evaluations,
medical judgments are made by an internist or pe-
diatrician and are based on information from auto-
mated multitest screening (adults), systematic laboratory testing and screening (children), a detailed health history, and a careful physical
examination. Individual medical problems are re-
corded, as are the services currently being received; the appropriateness of services being received is evaluated; and a judgment is made about
the services needed from primary physicians and
specialists, and about the need for drugs, aids,

and appliances. These judgments of unmet need are made for each problem and overall, for all problems.

Dental judgments made by a dentist are based on a dental history, on an examination of oral structures and on clinical assessment of oral hygiene, caries conduciveness, occlusion and alignment, periodontal status, oral lesions, and of decayed, missing, and filled teeth. Judgments are made about needs for extractions, fillings, bridges, dentures, dental specialist services, and dental health education. For each individual unmet needs judgments are then made for each problem and for all problems considered together.

Nursing judgments are made by a nurse based on data obtained through interviews with participants. The nurse judge determines whether the evaluees have problems which require nursing services to permit the evaluees (a) to maintain physical independence, (b) to carry out necessary treatments (therapeutic competence), (c) to have knowledge and understanding of existent medical conditions and (d) to carry out health maintenance practices. Ability to cope is taken into account in judging unmet needs for nursing services for direct care, for instruction, conselling, referrals and other supportive help.

The professional who makes judgments in the medical, dental and nursing areas tries to take a broad view of the individual in the context of his or her family unit and larger environment. Each professional looks for "all" need conditions (within his area of expertise) existing for the individual, and expresses each one of these by labeling from problem lists developed for use in each study component. A judgment is made about the care that should be received for these problems, details are obtained about the care actually being received, and the adequacy or appropriateness of this care is assessed. A professional judgment is then made about the individual's unmet needs for care and services for each problem. Finally, the professional looks at all the problems combined and makes a judgment about the individual's "overall" unmet needs: that is, "aggregate" unmet needs are assessed. Unmet needs

judgments for individual problems and for all
problems combined are expressed on ordinal scales.
In making judgments about unmet needs the professionals take into account problem severity
and the intensity and urgency of needs.

The unmet needs judgments which follow from
the examination and interview data are made by
persons normally practicing in the study area.
The "standards" and "criteria" applied to the
judgment process are those normally applied to
practice settings, as opposed to special, limited
standards established for study purposes. In
effect clinicians have been asked to do what they
routinely do with regard to assessment of problems
and needs, but to do this in a more structured,
systematized way and further, to record these
assessments. Then they go beyond what they
usually do by quantifying unmet needs. Judgments
of professionals seem reasonable bases for evaluating the health system where professional decisions dominate. For the medical components judgments on each individual are made by two physicians in order to provide a degree of "consensus
validity" to the findings. For all study components, a mechanism has been established in order
to get a quantitative measure of the reproducibility of the judgments.

The Meharry Medical College Study of Unmet
Needs is ambitious, global, and comprehensive in
its approach. It may have advantages, but also
limitations that relate to methods, study costs,
and interpretations of findings. First of all,
this study may be the first attempt to look at
unmet needs in similar population groups at two
points in time, in order to assess not only the
current levels of unmet needs but also changes
in unmet needs through time. It is one of few
attempts to relate unmet needs outcomes to particular models of care. The Meharry approach is
comprehensive in that it looks at numerous spheres
of potential needs. A comprehensive view of the
individuals being assessed is taken by looking
for "all" problem conditions within each of the
medical, dental, and nursing spheres. This
contrasts with approaches which focus only on
indicators or tracer conditions. After "complete"
problem lists have been developed, judgments of

levels of unmet needs are made about each problem
individually and then, within each of the medical,
dental, and nursing areas, about "overall" or
aggregate unmet needs.

From this work, the MEHARRY MONSAP - S scales
are derived. (5) These are a series of numeric
rating scales ranging from zero, indicating no unmet needs, to four, indicating great or urgent unmet needs. The ratings for the following separate
components are not combined in any manner, and
correlational factor analysis suggest that the
number of components of the scales cannot be reduced. For example, factor analysis of primary
phase I data suggests that high unmet nees for
dental care are not necessarily linked to high
levels of unmet needs for medical services.

For the individual evaluee the components of
the scales include:

M   medical primary practitioner services
O   oral-dental services
N   nursing services
S   specialty medical services
A   aids and appliances
P   prescription drug services

For the individual in his/her family and
neighborhood environment:

S   social indicators of well being based on
      reports from household interview on such
      variables as health, housing, neighborhood,
      education, income, job, family size and
      composition, and adequacy of health
      insurance.

For the study of Unmet Needs a comprehensive
approach was chosen because this seemed more relevant to program evaluation than just comparing
traditional morbidity and mortality statistics.(6)
As Elinson has noted, the inadequacy of traditional morbidity and mortality rates is "due in
part to the stagnation of total mortality rates
over long periods of time... to the increase of
chronic, non-infective disease... and to difficulties in determining the relationship of
mortality and morbidity."(7)

Unmet needs data, however obtained, are one of several types of "sociomedical" indicators which attempt to use factors other than biological states as measures of outcome. In addition to unmet needs indicators, the variety of sociomedical indicators includes measures of social disability, that is, the inability to perform a social role; and measures such as the "Sickness Impact Profile," which focus not on professionally defined disease entities but on behavioral expressions of sickness.

Many such indicators have been labeled "health status" indicators. *Unmet needs indicators, however, are not health status indicators, and to designate them as such is an error. Assessments of met and unmet needs for health care are not measures of the level of health of an individual or a population, but rather of the social capacity of the society to care for the sick. They measure the extent to which our present state of knowledge is being applied in a given population.* The quantification of unmet needs may be more helpful in many instances than concern with health status. Thus, for example, in a population of the aged, or of patients with hip fractures, or of patients with malignancy, a measure of unmet needs is the relevant indicator in determining the extent of the application of those health care measures which are possible and appropriate, given the present state of our health care knowledge.

Unmet needs indicators and health status indicators, though not the same, are related. One implicit assumption underlying the unmet needs concept, as applied in the Meharry study, is that the provision of appropriate health services according to need is an intermediate outcome of a health system whose ultimate goal may be to improve the health status of a population. Unmet needs indicators relate to appropriate services and resources which may be the inputs necessary to maintain or improve health status.

In spite of limitations a wide range of valuable information about population groups can be obtained through this method of assessing unmet needs and we feel that through applications in

other settings the approach can be refined so that
limitations of the approach are greatly reduced.
The following data are provided by such unmet
needs measurements:

(1) Data on the nature and extent of specific
    medical, dental, nursing, and health re-
    lated social problems existing in a
    population,

(2) Data on specific care received by problem,
    and appropriateness or adequacy of this
    care,

(3) Data on sources of care by major type,

(4) Data on barriers to care,

(5) Data on program characteristics including
    process and structure,

(6) Data on problems which are not being
    treated or which are being treated
    inappropriately.

    We assume that one objective of the health
system is to provide care according to need.
Determining what these needs are and how well they
are met would seem a highest priority input to
the planning of health services.

III. UNMET NEEDS MEASURES, THE NATIONAL CENTER
      FOR HEALTH STATISTICS, AND HEALTH SYSTEMS AGENCIES

    When we sought to develop our methods for
measuring unmet needs and changes in these
through time, in defined populations, quite
frankly many colleagues thought we were naive,
simplistic, and premature.

    In addition, critiques from economists
assured us that unmet needs were a bottomless pit;
to this latter we will return in the next section
of this paper. Further, when we met for two days
in late 1970, to seek help and advice from colleagues at the National Center for Health Statistics,
we asked what the National Center would do if
Congress asked for estimates of unmet needs for

care--which presumably could be linked to manpower and facility planning. We were at that
time advised - although colleagues were sympa-
thetic to our own plans - that the state of the
art was deficient for making such estimates.

It has therefore been gratifying to us that
an apparently meaningful way of assessing unmet
needs has grown out of the Meharry work and further, that evaluation of unmet needs for health
care has been incorporated as a component of
the Health and Nutrition Examination Survey
(HANES) of the National Center for Health Statistics. At present, the unmet needs component of
the HANES project focuses on a limited number of
index conditions and not on all aspects of an
individual's health. (8)

In an extraordinarily useful recently published document, Selected National Data Sources
for Health Planners, (9) the National Center for
Health Statistics presents data sources concerning general health statistics; morbidity, mortality and natality; manpower; facilities; use of
services; national health care programs; health
economics; and, demographic data sources. Implicit in these sources are their intended use under
Section 1513 (b) of P.L. 93 - 641, to assist
Health Systems Agencies with their mandated requirement to assemble and analyse data relating
to health status and its determinants, health resources and their use, and status of the health
care delivery system and its effects on use and
on health. (10)

Although cynics say that the Health Systems
Agencies represent old wine in new bottles, and
will soon show the same provider - dominated behaviors that led to the failures of the Comprehensive Health Planning legislation, even that
legislation had certain successes, and provided
both experience and awareness of the true capa-
bilities of health planning agencies at this
juncture in our history. (11)

The skyrocketing costs of health care, the
overproduction of short stay general hospital
beds, the failure of insurance to insure against

the costs of ambulatory services, the scandals
with nursing homes, medicare and medicaid, and
the fact that the United States is now spending
well over 8 per cent of its G.N.P. in the health
sector: al these factors taken together suggest
that P.L. 93 - 641 (or its successor) needs to
be taken seriously indeed both in the short and
long run.

van Dyke (12) has discussed the relationship
of federal and state entities to local Health
Systems Agencies under P.L. 93 - 641. Since these
agencies have to learn how to use quantitative
data and technology in order to plan, and since
with good will one has to assume that HSA's are
not being programmed for failure, it has to be
taken for granted that the federal government
wants states and local HSA's to have a data base
from which to plan; therefore, a national data
system has to evolve.

It is clear to us that there is an urgent
need to expand the fiscal resources and associated
capability of the Cooperative Health Statistics
System of the NCHS and to expedite the capability
to disaggregate data for specific areas: for example, by Health Systems Agency geographic area.
The data base used by the HSA's in planning should
largely be provided from federal and state
sources, augmented by special studies.

Alongside this we suggest that it may be
desirable to consider a major expansion and revision of the National Health Interview and Examination Surveys to include capability to generalize
to population sub-groups at and within Health
Systems Agencies areas.

Given that HSA's must collect data, that
unmet needs can be measured, and that unmet needs
data seem to be a logical basis for planning
services, we suggest that a major part of the
national data system which evolves should consist
of unmet needs data. Further, we suggest that
to accomplish this the content of the expanded
and revised NCHS survey should contain a more
extensive assessment of unmet needs.

A strong case can be made to include within the context of these revised surveys:

(1)   measures of primary sociobiological functions, the Activities of Daily Living (ADL) elaborated by Katz and Akpom; (13)

(2)   measures of equity of access to care, as elaborated by Taylor, Aday and Anderson; (14)

(3)   measures of unmet need using a modification of the Meharry - MONSAP - S Scales, as elaborated by Carr and Wolfe. (15)

Of course such unmet needs assessments would be expensive. However, the costs of all the work of the national health interview and examination surveys and of the federal health services research effort combined would be less than 1 per cent of the more than $600 per capita expenditures on health care in the United States in calendar year 1976. Further, any reasonable costs are bearable if better organized, meaningful and common data are thereby made available to those whose responsibility it is to plan health services.

IV.   UNMET NEEDS AND HEALTH CARE POLICY

It is, of course, foolish to believe that better data, including demonstration of levels of unmet need for specific health and health related services on the one hand, and wide gaps in equity of access on the other, would in some magical way lead to a more rational health policy, that would meet needs and narrow the gaps. But the position we take is that health policy should be based on facts, and should have as its goals the meeting of needs and equity of access to services.

It is further our contention that the strategy we have proposed in this presentation: linking needs assessments to the work of the NCHS and of the HSA's will quickly move us in the direction of a more rational approach to priority setting and allocation of resources from the local and regional levels upward to state and national levels.

Assessments of unmet needs lead not only to the identification of health problems which are not under proper care, but also to the identification of program deficiencies and defects if unmet needs are linked to sub-groups and to their sources of care. Also, as such uniform data are collected over time, inter-and intra-area differences and changes in unmet needs can be examined.

Again, we recognize that such data do not lead automatically to priority setting and to policy making. The data must enter into the political process. That process is one of conflict among special interest groups and lobbyists which usually results in major compromise, often based on disproportionate inputs from the world of corporate America. Conflict will occur with or without "good" data as input, and the allocation of health resources results. It is our contention that meaningful data on unmet needs and on equity of access will facilitate this political process and hopefully, lead to more rational and equitable allocation of resources.

Since, presumably,there is almost unanimous agreement that the track records of HSA's will prepare them for their role in resource allocation under National Health Insurance, the economics of health services using our approach of meeting unmet needs has to be questioned, as it would be by any classical or neo-classical economist. For example, Kenneth Boulding warns us that "one should be extremely suspicious of research devoted specifically to find out the need for medical care... 'needs'... are absurdly inflated... quantitative estimates of need... neglect the problem of demand and the problem of the price structure." (16)

And Victor Fuchs warns us that if there were compulsory insurance, and "the money price of the market - provided care goes to zero, people will tend to use the amount they would like to use if they were free to shift resources to satisfy other wants." (17)

Contrary to these opinions there is undeniable evidence that the demand for health services is finite and that it can be predicted with great accuracy for various sub-groups within the U. S.

population and for populations who are fully insured. Given the opportunity to have their needs
met, such "fully-insured" groups tend not to over-
use the health care that is available. Examples
of cases of "runaway" utilization are the exception and as already noted, use of services for
total populations is highly predictable in varied
settings such as the Canadian federal-provincial
health insurance programs, or in the National
Health Service of the United Kingdon, or in the
United States in the prepaid plans, in the Kaiser
and H.I.P. plans, and even in the Group Health
Insurance program of New York which operates
largely on a fee-for-service basis. There is
evidence, worldwide, that no more than 750 of
every 1,000 fully-insured persons use health
care services even once in a given year. A substantial number of the rest are casual users of
health care services. At the other extreme about
half of health services are used by less than 15
per cent of the population.

Thus, the attempt of health care programs to
meet needs does <u>not</u> open up a bottomless pit.
*People do not line up for health services as they
do for soft ice cream on a hot summer's evening.*

The problem is not that people are self-in
dulgent with respect to health care but rather
that there are often provider excesses in generating care for patients. Most health care services
are provider generated - the demand for health
services is not usually a so-called consumer
demand, but is provider - directed use of services
based on provider decisions about what is needed.
The abuses of provider - generated services under
medicare and medicaid, the numerous nursing home
scandals, have made us all increasingly aware of
the power of the provider to generate services
under any open-ended fee or reimbursement systems.

So a crucial part of the question of how to
meet unmet needs and enhance equity and appropriately contain costs and utilization, is less
that of controlling the voracious public's appe-
tites and behavior, than controlling those of the
providers of care. As unmet needs come to be
used as a basis for priority setting and resource
allocation, both health professionals and the

public must also be educated with respect to defining and meeting needs appropriately, and with
respect to issues of organization, cost, and prevention. Of course along with such education, controls and incentives on the provider side are man-
datory. These must include a strong peer review
system for both ambulatory and in-hospital services, alternative payment mechanisms which reduce the dependence on the fee system and on fixed
institutional reimbursement formulae, incentives
other than fee-for-service for ambulatory care,
home care, and outreach services, and disincen-
tives for inpatient stays.

If one posits that unmet needs data should be
the basis for priority setting and resource allocation to meet identified needs, the inclination
may be to try to meet these needs separately, in
isolated programs, or categorically. The United
States has long leaned to categorical health programs. We urge that this not be the outcome of
planning based on unmet needs assessments. Of
course some unmet needs in specific problem areas
may have greater priority than others and may need
to be dealt with in a focused way. However we
strongly feel that meeting of all needs, even
those of high priority, should be done in the context of a United States primary health care delivery system which is linked to specialty and super
-specialty back-up services. To reiterate this
important point, the use of unmet needs for planning services should not lead to further categorical assistance programs.

V.   SUMMARY AND CONCLUDING NOTE

We have taken the position that unmet needs
for health and related services can be measured in
a number of ways-some of these methods are admit-
tedly complex and relatively costly. The Meharry
Medical College approach to measuring unmet needs
involves health examination and professional
assessments and is being used for a long term
evaluation of the effectiveness of alternative
ambulatory health programs. Recognizing that if
the Meharry approach is to be used in other ways
and settings it will have to be modified and refined, we believe that the approach provides
meaningful unmet needs data which can be used as a

basis for planning. It is suggested that such
extensive assessments of unmet needs should be
made periodically for the United States population by the NCHS through a modified National
Health Examination Survey. With a modified
sampling procedure it would then be possible for
the NCHS to make unmet needs data available to
Health Systems Agencies for their specific service
areas. It is mandated that HSA's collect data
and determine needs of persons in their areas.
Data on unmet needs over time would be a relevant
type of data for HSA's to have available. Population-based unmet needs data can cover a wide
range of specific information including types of
specific problems existing within a population,
specific services received and particular resources and sources of care used. It also may
point to program deficiencies and barriers to
access to care. It can further indicate changes
over time in needs, met and unmet, within and between areas and sub groups. Other than the
specific findings of such assessments, they also
provide a basis for projecting and estimating
resource requirements.

The Meharry Medical College work has led to
a series of indexes which depict unmet needs along
multiple parameters. A single composite index
did not seem realistic or meaningful to us. In
fact, we feel that the search for a single number
which totally depicts a person's or population
health status or unmet needs status is like the
search for the Holy Grail - a futile search in a
complex and multifaceted area. (18)

The Meharry MONSAP - S unmet needs assessments, measure unmet needs for primary and specialty medical services, for nursing services,
for dental care, and for aids, appliances, and
prescription drugs, and place these needs into
the context of the social environmental circumstances. The indexes can be applied in toto or
in part in a variety of settings such as in specific HMO or group practice programs, in model
comprehensive care programs, or for HSA populations or sub groups.

The need for uniform national data is apparent. Further there is a growing social mandate

for health services to meet needs, (19) and for
the determination of health needs which are not
met to become a key priority of the fledgling
HSA's. Undertaking broad unmet needs assessments
on a national basis with the ability to break-out
HSA area data would cost far more than what is
now spent by NCHS on its Health Examination
Survey and by HSA's for the appropriate collection
and use of data. Yet the total cost would be a
pittance when compared even with the total expenditures in the health sector for other kinds of
studies.

A final word. The social indicator movement
can no longer be regarded as a fad. Social
scientists are developing concepts and measures
of societal change. (20) Perhaps the day is at
hand for the Executive Branch Council of Economic
Advisors to be expanded and modified to become a
Council of Social Science Advisors; in such an
expanded Council other voices in addition to those
of our economists would be heard, in order to link
societal changes and various social, including
health, indicators, towards the goal of meeting
the needs of our heterogeneous population more
appropriately.

ACKNOWLEDGMENTS

Thanks are extended to Vernaline Watson PhD,
of Meharry Medical College, for her inputs during
the thinking through of the content of this paper.
Dr. Jack Elinson as always, has been a firm and
constructive critic. Special thanks go to
Diane Northern MA of Columbia University who
prepared the manuscript.

REFERENCES AND NOTES

1. W. Carr and S. Wolfe, Int. J.Hlth. Serv.
    6,3 (1976).
2. J. Elinson (editor), Special Issue on Socio-
    medical Health Indicators, Int. J. Hlth. Serv.
    6,3 (1976).
3. D. G. Taylor, L.A. Aday, and R. Andersen. J.
    Hlth. Soc. Behav. 17, 1 (1976).
4. Much of the following description of the Study
    of Unmet Needs is adapted from W. Carr and
    S. Wolfe, op.cit.
5. The MONSAP - S Scales represent a revision and
    clarification of the scaling system used in
    the earlier reports of this study.
6. J. Veney, Inquiry. 10, 3-4 (1973).
7. J. Elinson, Social Indicators Research.
    1, 1 (1974).
8. National Center for Health Statistics. Vital
    and Health Statistics. Series 1, No. 10a and
    No. 10b. Plan and Operation of the Health
    and Nutrition Examination Survey, United
    States - 1971- 1973. U.S. Dept. H.E.W.,
    Washington, D. C., (1973).
9. National Center for Health Statistics.
    Selected National Data Sources for Health
    Planners. DHEW. Public. No. (HRA) 76-1236.
    Rockville, (1976).
10. Ibid. pp. iii - iv.
11. J. T. O'Connor. Mil. Mem. Fd. Quart.: Hlth.
    and Soc. 52, 4 (1974).
12. F. van Dyke. The National Health Planning
    and Resource Development Act of 1974 and
    National Health Insurance. A Discussion
    Paper for the Regional Medical Program Task
    Force. New York, (1975).
13. S. Katz and C. A. Akpom. Int. J. Hlth. Serv.
    6, 3 (1976).
14. D. G. Taylor, L.A. Aday, and R. Andersen.
    op. cit.
15. W. Carr and S. Wolfe. op. cit.
16. K. Boulding, in Economic Aspects of Health
    Care. J. B. McKinlay (editor), Prodist,
    New York (1973).
17. V. Fuchs, ibid.
18. T. W. Bice. Int. J. Hlth. Serv. 6, 3 (1976).
19. A. Donabedian. Benefits in Medical Care Pro-
    grams. Harvard Univ. Press, Cambridge (1976).
20. E. B. Sheldon and R. Parke. Science. 188,
    16 May (1975).

Future Directions in National Health Policy

4

Odin W. Anderson

I. The National Health Policy Tower of Babel

It is tempting to start and end this paper with the conclusion that a national health policy is meaningless unless
aspirations are reduced to a very few attainable objectives.
An overarching national health policy means too many things
to too many people and interest groups and attainable objectives have not been sorted out from utopian aspirations. The
health field has preempted religion as a form of secular sal-
vation from all pain, disease, disability, and death through
technology instead of last rites and suffers from the same
ecumenical confusion. The current range of proposed legislation for some form of national health insurance illustrates
this confusion. It seems to be assumed that there cannot be
a national health policy unless there is some form of national health insurance, particularly the Kennedy-Corman national health service type, within which more specific sub-poli-
cies are supposed to be rationally spawned. There is a fas-
cination with the seeming comfort of a security blanket of
a global national health policy, the more global the more
comfort.

To illustrate this confusion, to some a national health
insurance scheme (or a national health service) is intended
and expected to improve the health indicators of the American people; to others it is to cushion the burden of high
cost medical care episodes; to still others it is to restructure the main stream of the American health services in order
to make it more rational according to some self-evident concept; to all it is hoped that national health insurance will
slow, if not stop, the rising costs of health services. Per-
vading all aspirations is the now officially accepted value
that health care is a right with, as yet, no practical criteria as to what is an acceptable and possible level of proper access to services.

This paper was produced with the support of the Programmatic Grant HS 00080-11, National Center for
Health Services Research.

Still, there is the confusion as to whether good health is a right to be implemented or a commodity to be purchased. One or the other concepts implies vastly different social policy commitments through public means. We appear to be dazzled by the concept of right, but we are afraid to face this commitment forthrightly. I will return to this in due course.

Judging from experiences with national health insurance in other countries only two but important objectives have been attained, or more or less approximated; universality by compulsion to participate in the financing of health services, and in turn the right of access to specified services (but not necessarily the guaranteeing of supply), and the elimination of fear of costly episodes of illness. Implicit in national health insurance is another objective of having the costs of the health services shared so that the better off contribute more than the worse off. These were certainly objectives of the early national health insurance schemes in other countries. The objectives were to reduce the cost barrier at time of service and to share this cost equitably. It seemed to be taken for granted that health indicators would improve thereby although there was no explicit interest in them. The contemporary health services delivery system was to remain the same, or at least not expected to be unduly influenced by the financing method.

A possible exception may be the creation of the British National Health Service in 1946, but even here I believe it can be demonstrated that the primary interest was a "free" service and the structure that emerged was mainly the formalization of a delivery structure which was evolving for generations. The U.S.S.R. and Cuba, e.g., established their health services in a very different context by deliberately eliminating the vested interests such as they were which were counterparts more or less modelled on the western liberal-democratic health services delivery structures with intersecting public and private sectors and autonomous professions.

Now the western liberal-democratic national health insurance or health services systems are agonizing over rising costs, equal distribution of facilities, controls over use of services, and controls over quality. Further, they have discovered that a universal health insurance or service scheme has no measurable impact on the standard health indicators. The really notable achievements of universality, given the emerging egalitarian values, and the cushioning of costly illness episodes appear to sink into the background with the emergence of the other major concerns mentioned.

Now other countries are rationalizing that since, in general, a national health insurance has no measurable impact on mortality or morbidity rates the concept of governmentally financed and operated health service is thrown into doubt as a proper public policy. It is assumed, therefore, that now the objective of national health insurance is to improve the health of the people rather than cushion high cost episodes. The implication of this policy is to abolish public responsibility for funding and operating personal health services. There is plausible evidence that a general personal health services scheme does indeed, have little effect on the standard health indicators in affluent countries or at least throwing more money at it, (in post war-or-poverty terminology) will not improve them at the margin commensurate with the cost.

Forgotten seems to be the original objective of cushioning costs. Overlooked also is the fallacy of relying on the exceedingly crude health indicators as valid measures. It would seem reasonable to assume that with our high technology a few lives are saved for a while by organ transplants and other types of surgery, but there are not enough of them to affect the overall averages. (I am not necessarily referring here to heroic measures to continue life in prone and comotose individuals). Obviously, then, high technology procedures require a large critical mass of equipment and personnel which might not be otherwise used.

All countries are in a state of confusion regarding these issues, but in the United States it is even worse, because we do not even have the comfort of an umbrella of national insurance to give us the illusion that having one is in itself a national health policy. We are encountering all problems of debating national health insurance simultaneously whereas in the more simple days other countries were interested mainly in universality and cushioning of high cost illness episodes.

II. Let Heaven Wait

It might be salutary if this country would forget national health insurance for the indefinite future and concentrate on some well-selected hard core problems. There is the fallacious assumption that universal health insurance can be the vehicle for generating solutions for a variety of objectives such as raising health levels, containing costs, and distributing supply more equitably.

Other countries have demonstrated, as mentioned earlier,

that a universal health insurance or service in itself has
not accomplished these other objectives. Indeed, it tends
to obscure the fact that these intractable problems remain.
Comprehensive national health insurance is a bulldozer method rather than a pick and shovel method directed at specific objectives. The broad middle income groups are now in
favor of universal health insurance because they believe it
will correct the deficiencies in the existing health insurance benefits and improve the supply. Politicians are in
favor because they believe universal health insurance is a
cost containment method and a lever to restructure the
system.

There is an aura of equality about universal health insurance; everybody is in it and everybody benefits from it
and shares its costs. Given the fact that including Medicare possibly 90 percent of the population now has some form
of quite basic hospital and in hospital physicians' insurance,
it would seem that some type of overarching catastrophe coverage would cut across all income groups. The government
would, therefore, not need to commit itself to the open-
ended nature of a more comprehensive type of national health
insurance.

On the matter of health services delivery structures
it is unfortunate that the government has been so low-key
to help capitalize H.M.O. types of delivery in order to increase delivery options all across the country. Big buyers
of services could have some competitive options along the
general model of the Federal Employees Health Benefits Program. It is of interest that the great majority of Federal
employees choose the high option which is a higher cost to
the employee rather than the basic option matched by the
Civil Service Commission.

With a catastrophe coverage and a stimulus to competitive options as the general policy which are practical to
implement, for the sake of equity the low-income groups
should be targeted for rather comprehensive services bought
on their behalf from the main stream of the health services
delivery system including the increased range of options.
The low-income groups need "positive" discrimination, to
use a British term, because their incomes are lower and
their illness rates are greater than other groups in the
population. Targeted programs might improve health levels
for particular segments of the population. Federalizing
of Medicaid would facilitate standardization of eligibility
and benefits across the states and lift this tax burden
from the states and localities with its limited taxing power.

This will require an incomes test and the problem of stigma raises its ugly head.

The concept that health (and welfare) services be directed to the greatest need is hardly new, but it has labored under the awful stigma of the old poor law using an onerous and punishing means test. The Poor Law tradition pushed health and welfare programs to universality as a collective effort of a good society (1). What seemed to happen, however, is that universality over committed itself, and residual problems become under financed (2). The Medicare program in this country is illustrative. It is a catastrophic insurance scheme for high cost acute episodes among the aged rather than one for the hard core residual problems of long term and costly care of the chronically ill. These become the residuals that are ignored because the victims are a small minority and politically powerless. Stigma can be mitigated by making the eligibility purely objective in terms of family income and the raising the eligibility level from the currently ridiculous one of $4,500 a year per family to say, $10,000, around one-third of the families or 70 million people. Further, there should be realistic incentive to get doctors and facilities into underserviced areas. It would seem that doctors can be bribed to move to underserviced areas by paying them at least $75,000 a year. The physician supply is increasing. This kind of incentive would seem to be more in the American tradition than some kind of grudging penance service at a low price for a couple of years.

I would, therefore, attempt to make health care a right for high minimum income level, say, $10,000 and a commodity for the rest of the population, capped by a protective security blanket of catastrophe coverage for the entire population, details of which are politically negotiable. For catastrophe coverage there should be a variable coinsurance by income; the lower the income the lower the coinsurance graduated to zero. Further, I would target health problems that have a reasonable chance of showing improvements from the efforts. Examples are maternal and child health programs for areas with infant mortality in excess of say, 25 per 1,000 live births, extensive immunization programs, well-directed nutritional services, and services for controllable and curable diseases. Incurable diseases would come under the catastrophe type of security coverage.

As for methods and amounts of paying providers, I would not regulate hospital rates and physicians fees or salaries. They should be negotiable through prospective annual budgeting for hospital and fees and/or salaries for doctors. The current concept of reasonable and prevailing fees for doctors is a disaster and an anomaly as long as doctors are accorded a monopoly even if the supply increased markedly. It is obvious in this context that I would not regulate supply either.

I do not claim that these recommendations are original. Perhaps the combination is original. I am indebted to so many others that they are too numerous to document in a short paper.

III. Whose Utopia?

I have accused others of being utopian; obviously my recommendations are also utopian in that they are not currently politically acceptable. Consequently we wallow in a sea of incompatible objectives because the body politic seems to believe, that somehow, universality and comprehensiveness will more or less automatically solve rather than obscure the attainment of equality of access, control of costs, and equitable distribution of supply. These aspirations translated into a universal and comprehensive national health insurance scheme can result in a broad middle income hogging the resources. The poor and the underserviced will remain underserviced although ostensibly with a right that was not officially there before. What I am suggesting is a readjustment of the priorities for equity without universal national health insurance. This will not come about because the United States like all affluent countries are broad middle income countries and the poor and underserviced are residuals of the larger society with little political clout. I am, however, hardly arguing for a revolution in order to reduce the great majority of society to a low average instead, as in affluent societies, the great majority to a high average. The equity and, in fact, moral problem is one of dealing adequately with the poor and the politically powerless, without making all of us relatively poor and politically powerless.

In watching and studying the health services scene in this country and others, I am impressed with the exceedingly narrow range of policy options each country can ideologically and politically tolerate. Recommendations become conventional wisdom rather than well-coordinated health services implementation strategies with well-delineated objectives and methods. Consequently, I am driven to predict what will happen rather than recommend what should take place because policy determination is almost out of control of any faction, not to mention university professors. We cannot even decide operationally whether health care is a right or a commodity.

Characteristically we handle it as if it is both and overcommit ourselves to a universal and comprehensive health service which, given the American tradition we inherited from the British, will be underfinanced.

As an example of the global nature of official guides to policy, I refer to a recent publication of HEW entitled: Forward Plan for Health FY 1978-82, August, 1976. The report suggests that three criteria must be applied to the priorities established: 1) needed 2) doable 3) affordable. Then it goes on to say that a goal is to improve the health of the American people, and objectives are to assure equal access to quality care at reasonable cost, and to prevent illness, disease, and accidents (p.2). The three criteria of needed, doable, and affordable are understandably not specified. What is implied is that the political and administrative process will hammer out needed, doable, and affordable. Consequently, we ask for everything at the beginning and settle for a lot less. Near the end of a report there is a valid and sobering observation: "Activities directed toward the development of a more systematic conceptual framework for the analysis of the health domain are of very high priority, and are designed to increase our power to forecast and to predict the consequences of alternative policies." Further: "With respect to our health sector phenomena, we are a long way from being able to make such predictions with even a minimal degree of certainty." (p.14) Still, in the face of the description of the true state of affairs, an important faction in this country is espousing a complete national health service on the British model rather than target manageable problem areas as I have listed and described all too briefly.

IV. Countries Predetermine National Health Insurance Outcomes

Now what will happen in the United States? As stated earlier, the United States is facing a full range of problems simultaneously while considering universal national health insurance. Lacking a policy consensus politically, the United States is entertaining legislation which runs the gamut from a British-type national health service to a private enterprise insurance concept of covering high cost contingencies. The British-type enters into the very structuring of the system through the centralized funding mechanism. The contingency-type pays for high cost episodes and lets the delivery system evolve in a more or less market context. This is why there has evolved a range of delivery types in this country which is not true elsewhere. Given the variety of interest groups active, it is clear why there will be some middle-road initial legislation between these two extremes. I would hazard a guess that the mass of the public is more concerned with high cost episodes and relative conveniences of access at night and weekends than it is with reorganization of the system. The latter is a very technical problem which may well elude the general public, but high out-of-pocket costs and difficulty of access are salient (3). This does not preclude the need, of course, for the organizational changes to meet the public's dissatisfaction.

The following predictions are made:

1. Pluralistic funding will continue because of the reluctance to have public costs reflected in the national budget and the progressive income tax.

2. Universality will be debated and it is a toss-up whether or not there will be blanket coverage or more chopping off age groups like children. The aged are a precedent.

3. Private carriers will likely be intermediaries in the current Medicare arrangement in order to slow the growth of a federal bureaucracy.

4. It is very likely that at least some type of catastrophic insurance will be the easiest to pass. Medicaid will likely be federalized. The states find the burden onerous.

5. Simultaneously, there will be attempts to control the supply, particularly hospital beds. through regulation and involvement of the Planning Act PL 93-641. Planning will be negative rather than positive.

6. There will be continuing attempts to monitor physician decision-making in hospitals through PSRO, but the medical profession will control it (4).

7. The Planning Act PL 93-641 will create Health Service Areas for local interest group bargaining, but it will be loosely structured. Federal sanctions will be gentle.

8. The private insurance sector will continue to flourish even in the event of universal health insurance, because traditionally in the United States (as in Great Britain) financing will be tight. We inherited Britain's

> public niggardliness. The result may be a
> bulging of the private sector unless it is
> proscribed, an unlikely possibility.

9. Finally, the health system will continue to
    have a high technology emphasis disease by
    disease, e.g., renal dialysis. Priorities
    will be spontaneous rather than planned.

In sum, the American public is not familiar with a universal governmental system, and is unfamiliar with restrictions on resources and access like queues, and it does not have the civic consciousness to discipline itself as a collective. We are too diversified; there are too many strangers.

References

1. Well formulated in Richard Titmuss. Commitment to Welfare, London, Allen and Unwin, 1968.
2. See a sophisticated discussion in Robert Pinker. Social Theory and Social Policy, London, Heineman, 1971. (reprinted, 1973) p. 107 and throughout the book.
3. See Ronald Andersen, Joanna Lion, and Odin W. Anderson, "The Public's View of the Crisis in Medical Care: An Impetus for Changing Delivery Systems?", Economic and Business Bulletin (Fall, 1971).
4. Odin W. Anderson, "PSRO's, the Medical Profession and the Public Interest," Health and Society, p.379-388, (Summer, 1976).

Readiness of Sociomedical Sciences to Measure Health Status

5

Athilia E. Siegmann

Introduction

Health is not just an attribute of individuals, it is also a reflection of the social environment in which an individual experiences life, among which is the experience of health. How a society values and understands health will determine in great part how the individuals in society experience health. Even more - it will determine what society and individuals can do about health - how health will be measured and how the society's medical care services will be evaluated. At this point it is evident that the measurement of health status is viewed as a problem of social analysis.

There are certain measurement requirements that are necessary in order to both assess the health status of a population and to ascertain the relation of health services to outcomes in health status. The measures must be relevant to the phenomenon under assessment - health status, and they should also be relevant to the health problems of the society.

Our health status measurement strategies have mainly focussed on this latter criteria of relevance: relevant to the health problems of society, that is death, disease, disorder, dysfunction, discomfort, and dissatisfaction (1).

Health measurement strategy has had to compartmentalize or fragment aspects of health and has developed assessment protocols for physiologic and physical health problems, psychological or mental health problems, as well as for the social dysfunctioning attendent upon health problems.

This paper was prepared during the period that the author was on assignment as Technical Advisor, Office of the Director, DHEW-PHS-HRA, Bureau of Health Planning and Resource Development, Division of Planning Methods and Technology, Hyattsville, Maryland. The views expressed in the paper are the author's own, and in no way reflect policy or the position of the Government.

Health indicator measurement antedates most other social indicator measurement efforts. It has made many important contributions in its efforts. Nevertheless the health indicator movement still has not come to grips with a theory of population health formation from which to extract a health status indicator model.

In order to explain where we are today and where we still have to go in health status measurement, this paper will: 1) Trace the development of the relationships among health conceptualization, health problems, and health status measures that have taken place in the United States in the twentieth century, 2) the paper will also contrast and compare strategies for indicators that measure the health of a population and those that are used for assessment or evaluation of health services delivery programs, and finally there will be 3) presentation of a strategy for synthesis of the current state of the art, as well as use of the synthesis to develop a social system conceptualization of health formation that will serve as the basis for health status indicators that are more relevant to society's needs for measurement.

Development of Health Status
Measures in the Twentieth Century

The present century transformation of the United States' socio-economic organization from an agrarian society into a post-industrial society has been accompanied by three predominant disease patterns that have sequentially characterized different epochs of this period. In turn these patterns have been the infectious diseases, the chronic degenerative diseases of aging and the modern-life-style associated health problems.

Health Definitions

In order to understand and plan how best to amielorate or control disease problems a system of data designed to measure the population's health status is required. How health status is measured depends in large part on how health is defined. Sometimes the definition is implicit in the actions taken to measure health status, and at other times a formal health definition statement is the prelude to a measurement protocol. These definitions develop from the current context of the society's health problems as well as from the capacity of the society to solve them. Definitions have ranged from delimited concepts of health as freedom from disease to more expansive concepts that

include psychological and social functioning and feelings
of well-being and happiness.

Infectious Diseases

Measurement of health has been primarily influenced by
the activities and diagnostic classification of the medical
care system. Health status measurement is still influenced
by the early use of general death rates, age-specific death
rates, as well as death rates by specific disease categories
that were developed when infectious diseases comprised the
bulk of the nation's health problems. This is so even
though the "conquest" of these diseases has made them a
minor portion of the developed society's current health
problems. The infectious disease pattern still characterizes socially and economically deprived areas in developed
nations as well as developing societies lacking a preventive
health focus. When this is the case, outcome measures, such
as death rates, are appropriate for the social assessment
of acute and explicitly diagnosable diseases for which there
is a medical care therapeutic technology that has the capacity to alter the course of the disease and effect cure. In
this circumstance outcome measures are sufficiently sensitive to relate changes in health status to medical care, as
well as to account for the outcome. Those technologies that
are directed at the cause of the disease and which alter its
course and effect cures are called "high" technologies (2).
In these situations health status is a direct resultant of
receiving or not receiving therapy. Health status is
equated with receipt of services for the disease and with
its diagnostic label. The use of a direct measure of the
impact of sanitary and therapeutic care, the death rate,
simultaneously describes and explains health status. As
therapeutic techniques are more widely applied one can see
evidence of improvement in health status in the downward
trend of these rates for the population.

Acute Non-Lethal Diseases

In the period immediately following the conquest of
infectious diseases more persons live longer and are ex-
posed to the risk of acute non-lethal diseases. In this
situation morbidity measures of incidence and prevalence
serve the same function as death rates in explaining health
status. These morbidity measures are equatable with mortality measures, and both outcomes are linked directly to
medical care services. The implicit health definition that
characterizes this era is a view of health as freedom from
disease.

Chronic Degenerative Diseases of Aging

As the median age of the society increases the chronic
degenerative diseases predominate over infectious diseases
and acute non-lethal health problems. The content and impact of these disorders influence a view of health as the
capacity for role performance (3). Measurement strategy
accounts for the impacts of these illnesses and disabilities
by translating the impact into the time away from role performance. A variety of measures ensued from this view of
health. Initially a resource use dimension was operationalized. The sociological health surveys developed in the
1950's measured utilization of services and other resources
that served as proxy measures for the impact of medical
care techniques upon health status outcome. Use of services
served as proxy for cure. However, as social and economic
determinants also impact on outcome in these conditions,
utilization measures are compromised as assessors of population health status.

A temporal dimension was another early measurement
solution to the impacts of chronic disease. Undifferenti-
ated disability days due to illness were ascertained through
surveys of the populations. Either as counts or as part of
suggested global-type health indexes, they were used in an
attempt to account for the time involved in survivable
illnesses. With this view illness time is equatable to
productive time lost to the society from deaths. While
these disability measurements account for the temporal dimension of morbidity they neither qualify them nor qualita-
tively commensurate them to death (4).

A more sophisticated measurement strategy also evolved
from the use of survey instruments. The use of proxy measures in terms of degrees of physical dysfunction or degrees
of disabilities were linked to disease categories in the
studies of the Commission on Chronic Illness (5). Physical
dysfunction or physical disability can be measured objectively and are sensitive to illness changes. Function
measures thereby serve as indicators of the severity of
illness as well, as the changing course of illness (6).
They have been used to describe populations in terms of
basic biological and physiological function (7), and to
measure morbidity for total populations (8).

A more recent approach in this function and role performance capacity view of health is the Scaled Continuum
Dimension. Health is defined along a continuum from none
(i.e., death) to optimal (i.e., absence of disease or disorder). The continuum necessitates an equal appearing

interval scale upon which to place different degrees of illness and dysfunction. The methodology commensurates differentially rated function states and they are therefore
additive. Psychometric and utility scaling techniques have
been utilized. This is the social metric (9) that serves
as a valuation system for non-market activities analogous
to the market system dollar valuation. The Fanshel-Bush-
Patrick Health Status Index (10) has psychometrically
scaled preferences for function status levels used in the
index. These scaled and medically defined descriptive
functional levels are weighted by professional estimates of
future regressions (transitional probabilities) associated
with the dysfunctions.

Modern Life-Style Associated Health Problems

A more expanded view of health capacity for role performance in a social setting characterizes the health
definition of the measurement strategies used when disease
burdens shift to modern life-style associated health problems. René Dubos has proposed that "the nearest approach
to health is a physical and mental state fairly free of
discomfort and pain, which permits the person concerned to
function as effectively and as long as possible in the environment where chance or choice has placed him" (11).

A social definition of health has many interesting
measurement implications:

1. Factors other than medical care are determinants of
health in this view.

2. Consumer concepts of health emerge from criteria
relevant to physical activity levels, performance of
activities of daily living, physiological conformation,
degree of absence of pain and other symptoms, health-
producing behavior, and informational feedback from the
health care system (12).

3. There is implicit in the social definition of
health not only what input function it may serve to an
individual's endeavors, or what the state of health may be,
but also how it is attained (4, p.531).

4. In order to enable a complete assessment of health
status at the social definitional level it is desirable to
view both causes and effects simultaneously. A multivariate
social indicator model with health status as the outcome-
dependent variable is now a desiderata.

5. The indicator should be useful for the formal planning function of efficient resource allocation (13).

Health Status Indicator Strategies

Within the past ten years a general strategy has evolved to develop social indicators. This strategy seeks to provide society and decision makers with information about and the ability to monitor trends in the social domains of interest such as housing, education and transportation. The movement has not been characterized by successful input of its measurements into the decision making process. Partly this is due to the nascent stage of the movement and in part to the fact that indicators are still not derived from conceptually sound theories of social change (14), nor are the domain indicators interrelated to other areas of social concern (15).

The measurement strategy that has emerged in the social indicator movement has a tri-partite character. Typically a study includes a summary measure of all the domains that seem to assess a global perception of quality of life. In addition there is a perception of satisfaction with specific domains, and finally there is an attempt at in-depth examination of the determinants of satisfaction within the particular domains.

We have come a long way in the kinds of strategies that are used to develop health status indicators since the development of death rates. Today the basic strategy to develop an indicator of health status begins with the selection of measurement items that correspond to the researchers' distinct conceptualization or view of health in a specific dimension such as physical, or mental, or social health; or a combination of these. These scale items are either arbitrarily formulated by the researchers (16) or may be empirically derived from either consumer groups (17), patient groups (18), or professional groups (19), or a combination of these judgements (20) as to what items best characterize their view of the health dimension under assessment. After items are selected they are assigned a weighting or social metric (9) using either psychometric or utility scaling (21) techniques. Following an initial use of the scale it is further field tested to see if results are replicable - that is, how reliable is the measure. Its performance is also compared to external criteria to test if it does indeed measure what it has been designed to measure - that is, is the measure valid for the purpose at hand.

Disciplinary Research Indicators and
Policy Research Indicators

These health status indicator strategies may be part
of two distinct, but nevertheless overlapping and comple-
mentary, thrusts in current health status indicator construction. One is the development of indicators to
assess the health status of population groups, which I shall
refer to as disciplinary research based indicators. This is
in contrast to policy research wherein health status indicators are constructed to evaluate health action programs or
to measure the impact on health status of alternative health
policy decisions. The main distinction between these two
types of research is that the purpose of policy research is
to ascertain primarily how some specific aspect of the
health system impacts health status. Health status, per se,
is of indirect concern. The content of scales to measure
health status is directed at what it is that the medical
care system does - namely conservation of life and the care
and control of serious morbidity (22). This confines the
measurement effort primarily to physical health. Other
health components, mental and social health, may be included, but only on a secondary basis if at all. In
disciplinary research, where research problems arise from
issues identified in prior theoretical or empirical findings (23), the health status indicator is developed in response to a more basic and broader policy issue, the
assessment of population health for purposes of resource
allocation in the health sector. In this case, the selection of health components will be less a matter of elaborate
and detailed selection of items in order to pick up the
effect of a small programmatic change, and more, an empirical
assessment of the relative importance of the physical,
psychological or mental, and social components that comprise
the theoretical definition or formulation of health the researchers operationalize. In policy research, for the
purpose of evaluation, measurement scales have to be fine
tuned and detailed in order to sensitively pick up any
small effects or outcome changes in health status caused by
the innovation being assessed. On the other hand, health
status indicators for the purpose of population health
status assessment can be grosser scales. This is possible
as it is only necessary that individuals be distinguishably
assigned to discrete groupings along a continuum.

It is conceivable that the same or combinations of the
same health components can be included in either a health
policy research health status indicator or a disciplinary
research indicator. What most likely will not be the same

is the content of the items in their respective components.
Spirited arguments have been made for the inclusion of only
negative health items in these scales (13, p.514). Others
have persuasively advocated positive health items (24) as
well as items that capture vigor and well-being (25,26).
This argument is best resolved functionally in light of
the needs of the indicator. As health services are concerned with negative health or sickness, it would seem appropriate for policy and evaluative purposes to concentrate
primarily on negative items in the content of the components
of these health status indicator scales, whereas population
assessment instruments properly concern themselves with the
full gamut of experiential health.

Health Insurance Study (HIS), A Policy Research Indicator

In a study to determine the policy implications of alternative cost-sharing arrangements for medical care, the
Rand Corporation group at Santa Monica has constructed an
omnibus health status indicator instrument. An omnibus
scale is one that includes the three components of health -
physical, psychological/mental, and social. The researchers
are trying to see if having to pay more or less under different co-pay and deductible insurance schedules makes any
difference in the health status of the insured. John Ware
has described the rationale and content of the health
status indicator scales used in this social experiment. It
is a thoughtful discussion highlighting the requirements
that the health status indicator be sensitive enough to
discern the impacts of the differential demands for medical
care hypothesized in light of the different payment arrangements under scrutiny. The items selected for the scales
have to do mainly with conservation of life and prevention,
control and treatment of serious morbidity (22). Consequently, in the Rand indicator, measures of physical health
are stressed as well as the negative end of the physical
spectrum diseases, disorders, and dysfunctions. Psychological health and social health are a smaller proportion
of the total test battery and while items of well-being are
included emphasis upon negative-end of the health spectrum
items also applies in these three dimensions. The Health
Insurance Study indicators are broadly conceived profile
measures which although truncated for a specific purpose
will contribute greatly to the conceptualization, methodology and development of health status indicators for use in
direct assessments of population health. The necessity to
consider an empirical determination of both the relative
weighting for the components of health scales, and the range

in content along the health continuum of a component arises
if one considers the requirements that may form the desiderata for health planning. It is useful to consider these
policy implications of the research auspices of the indicator. If the indicator has been developed for purposes of
health policy evaluation then the likelihood is high that
any input function into decision making that the indicator
may have will be limited to decisions concerning manipulations in the health sector. On the other hand, an indicator
developed from the broader perspective of disciplinary research that is not limited to measures relating to health
sector determinants, has some potential to help guide
manipulations in sectors other than health. This is not to
say that these two types of indicators lack correspondence
or the capacity to contribute to each other.

Bridging Policy and Disciplinary Indicators, ADL and SIP

While a dichotomy has just been presented, in reality,
some health status indicator scales straddle these two research foci. A measure of primary sociobiological function,
the Activities of Daily Living Index (ADL Index) (19) is
useful for both evaluating the benefits of long-term
services for the chronically ill (27), as well as assessing
the health needs of a population (19,pp.503,506). The
hierarchical construct of this measure enables ranking of
persons for overall dependency in functional status with
reference to six sociobiological functions. Rankings are
made for bathing, dressing, toileting, transfer, continence
and feeding. This measure originated out of the need to
evaluate care for chronically ill institutionalized adults.
It has since been used to assess the health of children,
mental retardees, ambulatory sick, and noninstitutionalized
persons.

Another indicator, developed by Marilyn Bergner and
her colleagues, is the Sickness Impact Profile (SIP). The
SIP is a scale developed in an ambulatory care assessment
setting (20). It does, however, address the requirement
that the components and items be empirically rather than
arbitrarily generated. A unique feature of the items on
the scale is that they are the respondents' perceptions of
the impact of illness upon his or her behavior. Twelve
areas of living have been identified in the development of
the scale which directly generated the items by a lengthy
reiterative process of questioning persons in ambulatory
care with respect to how their illnesses affected their
behaviors. The twelve areas of living or categories encompass our three health components. The areas are: sleep
and rest, emotional behavior, body care and movement, home

management, mobility, social interaction, ambulation, alertness behavior, communication, work, recreation and leisure pastimes, and eating. As these are perceptions of behaviors this scale is relatively context free of direct reference to health problems and health services characterizations. The developers of the scale have advocated the use of the scale for cross-cultural comparisons. It is necessary, however, to consider that behaviors are culturally determined. Therefore some adjustments in scaling weights or SIP items would be necessary for such purposes. The two facts that, 1) the units of measure of the SIP are free of the context of the determinants of health while it still addresses the physical, psychological and social components of health and, 2) at the same time is developed from a social definition of health, make it particularly attractive as the construct to use in a causal health indicator model for assessment of the health of general population groups. While it still has not been used in this manner it lends itself to adaptation for this purpose.

The present form of the SIP presents a problem for use of the measure in surveys of a general population. The low frequency of illness-related behaviors that would occur on a given day in a general population in contrast to the frequencies that obtain in an ambulatory care setting may require that only those behaviors that are most prevalent in the ambulatory care setting be used. It has been suggested that "even reducing the number of sickness impact behaviors by two-thirds would result in a more refined measure of functional health status than is currently applied in population surveys" (28). It may also be necessary to extend the scale items to encompass positive health aspects if the scale is to be used for a broader conceptualization of health.

Bridging Policy and Disciplinary Research Indicators - MONSAP-S

The unmet health care needs indicator, MONSAP-S (29) that was developed at Meharry (30) is not a health status indicator. However, it is an example of an indicator that can settle in both policy or disciplinary research camps. While the indicator was developed for the purpose of evaluation of alternative delivery systems it has the potential for assessing the efficiency of the society in providing services deemed necessary for the health of the population. The cost of this elaborate protocol prohibits its use for general population assessment in its present form. However, for a general population the scales in MONSAP-S do not

require the detail and specificity that is needed to capture
all the changes needed to evaluate the relative efficiency
of different delivery systems. It also may not be necessary
to have ratings performed at the same professional skill
level as has been done at Meharry. It would be useful indeed if the Meharry methodology which is aimed at discern-
ing if populations do or do not receive needed care would
be compared to the results that are obtainable by using
the far less elaborate indicators of unmet needs and access
that have recently been developed (31,32,33). The Meharry
protocols could be used as validators of these far less
elaborate and inexpensive methodologies. It is hoped that
the announcement effect of these unmet needs indicators
will have the kind of impact on decision makers that will
redress the imbalance of distribution of health resources.
If they can at least point out and gain acceptance for more
efficient delivery systems a large contribution will have
been made. This is a very difficult area in which to effect
change as experience and evidence (34,35) have shown that
health resource distribution is not primarily a decision
made on the basis of needs but rather that health resource
concentration is a direct function of the society's distribution of wealth.

WHO Health Definition, Operationalized

     How often have we heard "health is a state of complete
physical, mental and social well-being and not merely the
absence of disease or infirmity"? (36) How regularly have
we immediately heard that it is an impractical utopian
World Health Organization definition that is neither useful
for goal setting or evaluation of health services; neither
is it useful for conceptualization of measures for health
status assessment (37). This criticism has been incorporated into health folklore and myth with the same rigorous
examination folklore and myths receive as they enter into
social awareness. Fortunately a busy group of researchers
in Alameda County in California have either been too busy
to hear this myth or else have with iconoclastic dispatch
set about destroying the myth.

     The research team felt that the WHO definition
"focussed attention on the living state rather than on the
categories of disease that may cause morbidity or mortality
....that life's....finer differentiation deserves attention-
not merely its existence and freedom from gross specific
disease" (38).

     The measurement strategy was to survey the population
sample and ask a series of questions from which indices of

physical, mental and social health were constructed. This
strategy is in the tradition of the sociological household
health surveys that preceded our psychometrically scaled
questionnaire survey instruments used today. This earlier
scale is a forerunner of the omnibus type HIS scale.

One of the interesting findings from the series of
studies of this group has been the positive relationship
between desirable personal health practices and longevity.
The good health practices identified were: seven to eight
hours sleep, sufficient exercise, eating breakfast, and
moderation in cigarette smoking and eating and drinking.
These health habits were not highly intercorrelated, but
they did have a cumulative effect on mortality reduction.
What is most interesting is the fact that the observed relationship between mortality and health practices is
independent of income and current health status (39) as
assessed by the three health component scales.

The Human Population Laboratory conceptualization of
health is closest to a disciplinary research context than
any of the indicators previously described. There is a
distinct contribution to methodology in the relationships
that were found between some of the health components.
There is evidence now for positive correlations between
physical and psychological health as well as positive correlation between social and psychological health. The
interest of investigators in examining the relationships
between components of health and between different scales
that purport to measure the same component is still to be
stimulated. The Rand HIS study is one of the few that has
begun to look at scales simultaneously. The Lawrence County
Health Care Project in Moulton, Alabama has also focussed
on the cross-sectional and longitudinal study of health
measurement instruments (40). However, there is still much
to be done in a meaningful way, in establishing relationships between health components and seeing how different
measures compare in the assessment of a population's health.

These comparisons and contrasts between policy based
research and disciplinary based research, as well as the
few illustrations, have been presented to give an indication of some of the methodologic aspects of the work in
indicators. In October of 1976 a conference on Health Status Indicators organized by Dr. Martin Chen of the DHEW -
Human Resources Administration - National Center for Health
Services Research, was held in Phoenix, Arizona (41). The
presentations at the conference revealed the great degree
of sophistication in scaling methods, statistical techniques, and content operationalization of scales that has

taken place in the past 5 years since the previous conference on health status indicators (42).

Towards an Epidemiology of Health

While factor analyses (43) have indicated evidence for
a global health factor as well as evidence for distinct
components that make up an omnibus scale, there is still no
consensus on what it is that health scales measure, or if
in fact they do fully measure health and not merely selected
aspects of health. This conceptual problem does not arise
when the etiology of disease is to be ascertained. The
whole armamentarium of epidemiologic research is brought to
bear upon the question. It has been quite a challenge to
search for a study or any study of the epidemiology of
health. Defining epidemiology as the study of the distribution and determinants of disease (or the phenomenon in
question - health) in man (44), it was rewarding to come up
with one title "The Epidemiology of Health" by Margaret
Merrell and Lowell Reed, a paper presented at the New York
Academy of Medicine, Institute on Social Medicine in 1947
(45). It is a five page paper that by analogy to the epidemiologic method of observing unattacked as well as attacked individuals when assessing a disease phenomenon
makes a telling case for an epidemiologic investigation of
health.

The particular need for a classification system that
can be used to relate the classes of health status to other
determinant variables is identified,as well as the fact
that these studies will yield some of the basic information
necessary for planning medical care programs. The authors
expressed confidence that with the use of surveys that were
then already instituted, and with the 1947 movements toward
comprehensive medical care that made provision for the examination of "whole" population groups rather than only ill
persons, the beginning had been made to collect the basic
data which would allow the study of the epidemiology of
health. Thirty years later it is surprising that we have
developed sufficient sophistication in the extremely complex and costly business of health status indicator scale
construction, to again at a forum sound the challenge that
Merrell and Reed issued in 1947.

They had postulated that the development of a classification system for health status would be much more difficult and take many more attempts than was the case for
disease classifications. We are now at the stage where the
"descriptive" epidemiology (27,p.481) of health can begin

to be formulated. This is the development of the classification system. It is the health status indicator system
which will describe the distribution of the phenomenon of
health. The previously mentioned investigations of
Breslow, Ware and Miles that have begun to examine relationships between component health scales and between
different scales that measure the same component is the
necessary first stage to get an acceptable classification
system which will enable observations to be made and thereby describe the distribution of health. In this way a
descriptive epidemiology will be in place. By the very
nature of its comprehensiveness and interrelatedness this
is a task that will require a substantial investment of
time and money. It has to be done in a coordinated fashion,
and most likely will require cooperation among the specialists in different locations in the health status indicator
research community as well as requiring financial support
and some form of coordination assistance from the National
Center for Health Statistics and the National Center for
Health Services Research.

    The second phase in developing the epidemiology of
health is to search for the determinants of the observed
distributions. This is the "analytical" epidemiology (28,
p.481) that will have to be developed if health status
assessment is to serve the rational process of resource
allocation for the purposes of health planning. This will
require the use of health status indicator multivariate
models in assessment of the role of the determinants of
health. This area has also begun to be developed (46,47).
It may be somewhat optimistic to say that all the pieces
for this next thrust are available and that with a supported
coordinated effort the ambitions of Merrell and Reed can be
realized. This is not to say that an epidemiology of
health can be developed quickly. Development time for some
of our current new scales has been more than five years.
This new task also will be a slow and reiterative process,
but it is one that can, and should, be done.

A Time Trend: Global Health Perception

    Another allied task that should be considered is the
establishment of a time series for a global perception of
health status. Since the 1950's when the sociological
household health surveys were instituted, health status has
been assessed by the global question that asked individuals
for a simple perception of their health, e.g., "would you
say that your health is excellent, good, fair, or poor
today?" The value of this type question is increasingly

appreciated. In large questionnaire batteries it often
correlates best with the whole battery. While it may not
be as stable an item as physical or social dysfunction it
has the same virtue of all scales of perceptions of health,
namely it is relatively free of the context of the structure, processes and diagnoses of the medical care system.
It would be a useful monitor that could be established by
using results from past surveys and replicating the questions in future surveys. Such a trend series would help
tie together a consumer definition of health with a conceptualization of a general underlying health factor.

Summary

In this discussion of health status indicator measurement we have seen that research and methodologic strategies
will be dependent upon the purpose the indicator is to
serve. While policy research and disciplinary research
select out different items to operationalize components of
health, there is much correspondence and developmental ex-
change between these two research foci in construction of
health status indicators. The ultimate need for health
planning for indicators that will serve rational resource
allocation purposes may best be met by investment in a
program to study the epidemiology of health. It has been
suggested that a time series be established for a global
perception of health status.

Acknowledgements

I would like to thank Marilyn Bergner, Margery Braren,
Harold Dupuy, and Sally Guttmacher for their helpful comments on earlier drafts of this paper, and Hannah Frisch
for preparing the copy for publication.

References

1. J. Elinson, in Handbook of Medical Sociology, H.E.
    Freeman, S. Levine, and L.G. Reeder, Eds. (Prentice-
    Hall, Inc., Englewood Cliffs, N.J., 1972), pp.488-490.

2. L. Thomas, New Engl. J. Med. 285, 1366 (1971).

3. T. Parsons, in Patients, Physicians, and Illness, E.
    Gartly Jaco, Ed. (Free Press, New York, 1958), p.168.

4. A.E. Siegmann, Int. J. Hlth. Serv. 6, 521 (1976).

5. Commission on Chronic Illness, Chronic Illness in the
    United States, Vol. IV, Chronic Illness in a Large
    City. (Harvard University Press, Cambridge, Mass.,
    1957).

6. S. Katz, A.M. Ford, T.D. Downs, and M. Adams, Med.
    Care. 7, 139 (1969).

7. C.A. Akpom, S. Katz, and P.M. Densen, Med. Care. 11,
    121 (1973).

8. U.S. National Health Survey, Chronic Conditions
    Causing Limitation of Activities, United States, July
    1959-June 1961. Public Health Service Publication No.
    584-B36, Series B. No. 36. (Washington, D.C.,1962).

9. D.L. Patrick, Int. J. Hlth. Serv. 6, 443 (1976).

10. M.M. Chen, J.W. Bush, D.L. Patrick, Policy Sciences,
    6, 71 (1975).

11. R. Dubos, in Health and the Social Environment, P.M.
    Insel and R.H. Moos, Eds. (D.C. Heath and Co.,
    Lexington, Mass., 1974), pp.439-450; Also in Man
    Adapting (Yale University Press, New Haven, Ct., 1965),
    pp.346-361.

12. J.D. Hennes, Med. Care Rev. 29, 1268 (1972).

13. T. Bice, Int. J. Hlth. Serv. 6, 509 (1976).

14. C.Y. Glock, Science. 194, 52 (1976).

15. J. DeNeufville, Social Indicators and Public Policy.
    (Elsevier Scientific Publishing Company, Amsterdam,
    1975).

16. S. Fanshel, and J.W. Bush, Operations Research. 18, 1021 (1970).

17. J.D. Hennes, A consumer oriented strategy for the measurement of health. (Planning and Evaluation Unit Colorado Department of Education, State Office Building, Denver, Colorado, November 1973). Mimeograph.

18. B.S. Gilson, J.S. Gilson, M. Bergner, R.A. Bobbitt, S. Kressel, W.E. Pollard, and M. Vesselago, Am. J. Pub. Hlth. 65, 1304 (1975).

19. S. Katz, and C.A. Akpom, Int. J. Hlth. Serv. 6, 493 (1976).

20. M. Bergner, R.A. Bobbitt, S. Kressel, W.E. Pollard, B.S. Gilson, and J.R. Morris, Int. J. Hlth. Serv. 6, 393 (1976).

21. G.W. Torrance, Toward a utility theory foundation for health status index models. Prepared for the Health Status Index Conference, Phoenix, Arizona, October 25-28, 1976. Sponsored by the National Center for Health Services Research, U.S. Department of Health, Education, and Welfare. Forthcoming in Health Services Research: Supplement.

22. J.E. Ware, Jr., The conceptualization and measurement of health for policy relevant research in medical care delivery. Paper delivered at the 1976 annual meeting of AAAS, Boston, Mass., February 1976.

23. J.S. Coleman, Policy Research in the Social Sciences. (General Learning Corporation, Morristown, N.J., 1972).

24. M. Jahoda, Current Concepts of Positive Mental Health. (Basic Books, New York, 1958).

25. N.M. Bradburn, The Structure of Psychological Well-Being. (Aldine Publishing Co., Chicago, 1969).

26. H.J. Dupuy, Developmental rationale,substantive, derivative, and conceptual relevance of the General Well-being schedule, 1973, working paper.

27. P.M. Densen, Amer. J. Epi. 104, 478 (1976).

28. A.E. Siegmann, and J.Elinson, Med. Care. 15, 83 (May 1977).

29. The respective components of the MONSAP-S scales are:
M – medical primary practitioner services, O – oral-
dental services, N – nursing services, S – specialty
medical services, A – aids and appliances, P – prescription drug services, and S – social indicators of
well-being (in the examinee's environment).

30. W. Carr, and S. Wolfe, Int. J. Hlth. Serv. 6, 417
(1976).

31. D.G. Taylor, L.A. Aday, and R. Anderson, J. Health
Soc. Behavior. 16, 39 (March 1975).

32. L.A. Aday, Med. Care. 13, 447 (June 1975).

33. D. Hewitt, and J. Milner, Med. Care. 13, 928
(November 1975).

34. V. Navarro, Med. Care. 12, 721 (1974).

35. V. Navarro, Bull. N.Y. Acadamy Med. 51, 199 (1975).

36. Constitution of the World Health Organization, in The
First Ten Years of the World Health Organization.
(World Health Organization, Palais des Nations,
Geneva, 1958), p.459.

37. S. Goldsmith, Hlth. Serv. Reports. 87, 212 (1972).

38. L. Breslow, Int. J. of Epidemiology. 1, 347 (1972).

39. N.B. Belloc, Prev. Med. 2, 67 (1973).

40. D.L. Miles, Health care evaluation project. Moulton,
Alabama: Lawrence County Health Care Project
(unpublished).

41. Proceedings of the Conference on Health Status Indicators, Phoenix, Arizona, October 1976. Hospital
Research and Educational Trust, Chicago (forthcoming).

42. R.L. Berg, Ed., Health Status Indexes. (Hospital
Research and Educational Trust, Chicago, 1973).

43. J.E. Ware, G. Miller, and M.K. Snyder, Comparison of
factor analytic methods in the development of health
related indexes for questionnaire data. Carbondale,
Illinois: Southern Illinois University School of
Medicine Technical Report No. MHC73-1, 1973.

44. B. MacMahon, T.F. Pugh, and J. Ipsen, <u>Epidemiologic Methods</u>. (Little Brown and Co., Boston, Mass., 1960).

45. M. Merrell, L.J. Reed, in <u>Social Medicine: Its Derivatives and Objectives</u>, I. Galdston, Ed. (The New York Academy of Medicine Institute on Social Medicine, 1947; The Commonwealth Fund, New York, 1949).

46. The rationale for an epidemiology of health is one of the best arguments for the development of positive end of the spectrum and well-being items for inclusion in each component of health in the indicator. There is a need also for empirical derivation of items that are elicited from consumers' concepts of what health is or how it is experienced.

47. The validation of a disciplinary research based health status indicator lies within the epidemiology of health.

6

The Measurement of Psychological Well-Being

Norman M. Bradburn

In this paper I would like to review attempts to develop measures of psychological well-being for use in the general population and then comment briefly on the state of art at the present time (1). In reviewing past studies I shall of necessity be selective, the selection being a subjective one based on those studies that I have found to be particularly useful in advancing the state of the art. Needless to say, others reviewing the same literature might well focus on other studies or other approaches altogether.

Before discussing the development of empirical measures, let me consider what it is that we are trying to develop measures of. The reader will no doubt have noticed that I titled my paper, "The Measurement of Psychological Well-being" rather than the measurement (or assessment) of mental health or mental illness. It would take us far beyond this symposium to consider fully the meaning of terms such as "mental health" or "mental illness" and whether or not it is appropriate to use a health/illness model in discussing mental life. While I think that it makes some difference whether or not one conceptualizes the phenomenon we are studying as a health question or as a question of interpersonal behavior, I shall try to show that for the purposes of measurement, it appears to make little difference whether one thinks that one is studying mental health, mental illness, psychological well-being, general well-being or personal adjustment, to pick a few of the terms that have been applied to the measures we shall be talking about. The conceptual differences are less important to the content of the measures than to the way in which different measures are thought to relate to one another and, perhaps most importantly, to one's belief about causative factors. Since we are concerned here with measurement of current states rather than etiology, we shall happily sidestep that quagmire.

One of the first scales developed for use with large, if
not exactly general, populations was that which came to be
known as the Neuropsychiatric Screening Adjunct, developed, I
believe, primarily by Shirley Star, working in that brilliant
group of social scientists put together by Samuel Stouffer
during World War II to help with a variety of human problems
that arose in the armed forces during the war (2). The
problem that confronted the research team was a formidable
one. A large number of young men were being inducted into
the army rapidly. A small, but unknown, proportion of them
had mental problems that would disqualify them from duty.
The only known way at that time to detect men with these
problems was a lengthy examination by a psychiatrist. The
number of psychiatrists available to the army was far too
small to interview everyone being inducted, so some measure
had to be developed that would screen out those who were the
most likely to have problems, and then have the psychiatrists
interview only those men.

Notice that measurement here was a two step process.
First, there was a paper-and-pencil test that could be easily
administered in large groups at low cost. On the basis of
the responses to the paper-and-pencil test, a smaller group
was selected who were then interviewed by medical officers
(psychiatrists) to make a final determination of medical
status. Empirically, the test items were developed so as to
maximize the discrimination between the "well" and the
"psychoneurotic" where "well" and "psychoneurotic" were
defined by the psychiatric determination based on a personal
interview. The test was successively refined and a usable
version was developed that had a reliability of about .85
and was capable of screening out a group about 80% of which
were finally diagnosed as psychoneurotic and rejected for
psychiatric reasons.

It is particularly interesting from the vantage point of
today to look at the type of items that went into the Neuropsychiatric Screening Adjunct. The authors adopted a rather
eclectic theoretical stance in the initial selection of
items. The items reflected both a concern for what the
individual's childhood had been like (reflecting an implicit
causative theory) and on recent functioning. They inquired
about 15 separate areas of life, 8 of these were related to
aspects of personality development, 5 were related to present
functioning, and 2 to what they called "war motivation",
specifically identification with the war effort and acceptance of the soldier role.

While there is no need here to go into the details of
the final construction of the scale, it is worthwhile men-

tioning the 5 areas of current functioning that suggested
themselves to the authors as a focus for questioning because
they are to a considerable extent those that are still used
today. The 5 areas were 1) sociability, that is liking for
and association with other people; 2) worrying--good adjustment implied a lack of worry about one's self and the future;
3) oversensitivity defined by such traits as irritability,
quickness to take offense, and resentment of criticism; 4)
personal adjustment as measured by self-confidence and a lack
of self-pity, depression and anxiety; and 5) psychosomatic
complaints such as vague physical complaints like "nerves",
stomach trouble, insomnia. There were similar content areas
relating to childhood experiences.

For all of the differences in conceptualization and
detail of particular questions, it is striking how similar
today's measures of well-being are to the general content
areas first developed by the researchers in Stouffer's group.
This similarity is, of course, due in part to the fact that
general conceptions of personal adjustment have not changed
much since then. But it is also due to the influence that
the researchers involved in The American Soldier series have
had on the development of empirical social sciences in the
post-war period.

After the war, in the 1950's, there was considerable
interest in social psychiatric studies relating environmental
stresses and supports to rates of mental illness. In particular I have in mind here the Stirling County studies and the
Midtown Manhattan studies (3,4). Such studies required the
estimation of rates of psychiatric impairment in populations
living in environments that differed in ways thought to be
related to mental illness. Here again practical requirements
of manpower and cost required the development of measuring
instruments that could be administered by non-medically
trained personnel. The research design called for sample
surveys of defined populations.

The research strategy adopted in these studies was an
adaptation of that used in The American Soldier. Instead of
using the questionnaire as a screening device to select those
who would then be interviewed more intensively by psychiatrists, an interview schedule was developed that became the
proxy for the psychiatric interview. In effect the types of
questions that would have been asked by a psychiatrist in
diagnostic interviews were put into a structured form that
could be asked by different interviewers in a home interviewing situation. Because the interview was seen as a proxy for
an interview with a psychiatrist, the researchers did not
follow entirely the path of the army researchers and use a

completely pre-coded standardized questionnaire that could be
administered by any trained interviewer. Instead they chose
an intermediate strategy, using a structured but still sub-
stanitally open-ended interview schedule and relied on allied
professions such as social workers, psychologists and other
social scientists to do the interviewing. The completed
questionnaires were read by two psychiatrists. Each respondent was given a psychiatric impairment rating on a 7-point
scale independently by each psychiatrist. The two ratings
were then combined to yield one overall impairment score for
each individual.

We can see these studies as a phase in the development
of the methodology of measuring mental health. While The
American Soldier researchers had solved the manpower dilemma
by reducing the pool of individuals that needed to be interviewed by psychiatrists through the use of a psychometrically
sophisticated screening device, the social psychiatry studies
retained the method of a lengthy interview with each individual regardless of his probable health status, but modified
the interview so that it was more structured and could be
conducted by social scientifically trained, but not necessarily psychiatrically trained personnel. The interview protocols provided the raw data which was then used by psychiatrists to make a judgment about impairment. While some
attention was paid to the reliability of the ratings between
the two judges, little attempt was made to treat the data
from interviews in quantitative form, although Leighton, et
al do report that a scale derived from the interviews in
Stirling County correlated highly with the psychiatrists'
ratings and that substantially the same empirical results
would have been obtained by using such a scale instead of
psychiatric ratings (3). The psychiatrists' ratings of
impairment, however, were the measure that resulted from the
interviews and was subsequently used in the analysis of
differences among socio-economic groups and those living in
different environments.

The next logical development in measurement was to
dispense with the direct psychiatric ratings altogether and
use quantitative scores derived from interviews as the measure. This step was taken by Gurin, Veroff and Feld at the
Survey Research Center of the University of Michigan,
reported in Americans View Their Mental Health (5). At the
same time they extended the scope of the population of
interest to that of the non-institutionalized population of
the United States. What we have in this study is the merging
of two research traditions. On the one hand, we have seen
the development of a body of content that has come to define
in a rough fashion what is meant by mental health or personal
adjustment or psychological well-being, whatever name you

wish. This set of indicators, imprecise as they may be, grew out of the psychiatric literature and was more or less validated using traditional psychiatric diagnostic interviews. On the other hand, we have the sample survey techniques developed in the measurement of public opinion. These techniques, which employ personal interviews with individuals selected through probability sampling methods, were easily adapted to interview content that had been developed from the studies using psychiatric ratings.

While the Gurin, Veroff, and Feld study reflected the past history of the field in the content of their questions, they did extend and elaborate somewhat the content areas and partially shifted the focus of attention away from childhood experiences toward current functioning. They extended the personal adjustment indicators used by Stouffer and his colleagues to include more on mood and general happiness, and they differentiated adjustment within different important life roles that people play, that of work, marriage, and parenthood. Physical symptoms, psychological symptoms of anxiety and indictors of self-esteem continued, however, to be important indicators of mental health.

My own work came shortly after the Gurin, Veroff and Feld study and was considerably influenced by it both in method and content (6,7). Like them, we relied on structured, almost entirely pre-coded questionnaires with personal interviews (although in some cases self-administered) conducted by ordinary survey research interviewers who had no professional training in social sciences or psychiatry. While the content of the items reflected heavily the measurement tradition I have described, construct validity was demonstrated through internal analysis, as was the case in the Michigan study. Our studies extended the methodological development in two ways: First, we went one step further in the direction taken by Gurin, Veroff and Feld and focused entirely on current functioning. The content areas were still similar to those suggested by Stouffer, et al but the questions were now phrased almost entirely in terms of current feelings states, adjustment in present major roles, present social relations, symptom experiences in the recent past and current self-conceptions. Second, reflecting the concern with response bias and "yea-saying" bias that had permeated the literature in psychology during the late '50's, we phrased some of the questions in a positive rather than a negative direction, asking not only about negative feeling states but also about positive ones. That small change had surprising results.

In the pilot study conducted in four small towns,

respondents were asked whether they had experienced several
feeling states during the preceding week (6). The list of
feeling states asked about had been chosen to balance
positive and negative feelings. For example, we asked
respondents how often during the past week they had felt
"bored" or "on top of the world" or "lonely" or "proud
because someone had complimented them on something they had
done." Analysis of the data indicated that the items fell
into two clusters--one indicative of positive affect and the
other indicative of negative affect. This finding in itself
was not so surprising since we had anticipated that the two
sets of items would be positively intercorrelated. What was
surprising, however, was that the two clusters did not
correlate negatively with each other; there was a zero
correlation between them. Thus it was impossible to predict
an individual's score on the negative affect dimension from
knowledge of his score on the positive affect dimension and
vice versa.

On the other hand, both dimensions were related in the
expected direction to overall self-ratings of happiness or
subjective well-being. The best predictor of the overall
self-rating was the discrepancy between the two scores: the
greater the excess of positive over negative affect, the
higher overall rating of psychological well-being.

The fact that the discrepancy between positive and
negative affect should be the best predictor of overall
happiness is, of course, similar to older pleasure-pain
models. Where this particular conceptualization differs from
more traditional ones is found in a further finding. The
data from the pilot study indicated that not only were variations in positive and negative affect independent of one
another but that, on the whole, the two clusters were correlated with different variables. In most general terms, it
was found that the variables which were related to the
presence or absence of positive affect had no relationship
to the presence or absence of negative affect, while the
variables which were related to the presence or absence of
negative affect had a similar lack of relationship to positive affect. More specifically, the negative affect cluster
was related to items reflecting psychosomatic symptoms,
anxiety, poor role adjustment and worries--all traditional
indicators of poor mental health. On the other hand, the
positive cluster was related only to items reflecting social
involvement, sociability and active involvement in the world
around one. Sociability was one area of functioning that had
been in the original Stouffer, et al screener and had been
retained in almost all of the subsequent studies, but had
continued to show relatively low relationships with more

global ratings of mental health. In our studies, it showed up as a separate area that related only to positive affect.

The implications of these findings for research on psychological well-being has been elaborated elsewhere and need not concern us here (7). Suffice it to point out that these data suggest that a simple unidimensional rating scale may not be sufficient to measure psychological well-being. Or even if we get a single scale that is satisfactory for most purposes, it may conceal as much as it reveals.

The culmination of these developments will be the development and validation of a scale measuring psychological well-being that can be administered routinely to samples of the U.S. as part of the National Health Survey program. Such development is currently underway at the National Center for Health Statistics and a preliminary version of a scale measuring general well-being has been administered as part of the Health and Nutrition Examination Survey (8). While it differs in specifics, NCHS's general well-being scale reflects the experience of researchers discussed here. It is a wholly pre-coded questionnaire that either can be administered by an interviewer or can be self-administered. It focuses entirely on current functioning, questions being asked in terms of feelings or experiences during the past month.

The measure being developed by NCHS has two major content areas; one indicating overall general adjustment and the other tapping direct expression of psychological distress over the past year at the time of the examination. The first part, which is more similar to the measures we have been discussing, has 6 sub-scales. These sub-scales are called: positive expressions of general well-being; energy level; emotional-behavioral control; depressed vs. cheerful mood; tension-anxiety state; and health worry and somatic distress. The scales have been refined to improve their internal consistency and undoubtedly will undergo further statistical refinements before they are put in final form.

Encouragingly similar results have recently been reported by Schuessler and Freshnock based on tests that have been developed in a sociological rather than explicitly psychological tradition, although the influence of The American Soldier studies has been strong on sociology as well as psychology, so one cannot say that they are in fact independent traditions (9). Scheussler and Freshnock constructed an interview schedule of 107 items from 31 separate scales that have appeared in the literature since 1936. All of these scales were concerned with the broad area of

psychological well-being, although they appeared under a
large variety of names and include some items from the studies I have mentioned. They administered this questionnaire
to a nationwide probability sample of individuals by personal
interview using ordinary survey interviewers. They factored
the responses and obtained 8 independent factors. They
titled these factors: pessimism, depression, social cynicism, anxiety, inefficacy of the individual, job morale, life
satisfaction, and social vitality. These 8 factors map
fairly well onto the 6 sub-scales in the NCHS measure. The
major differences would appear to be a function of the
theoretical orientations of the authors. Those tests that
derive from the sociological tradition have factors reflecting attitudes toward society (e.g., cynicism about government
and trust in others) and more specific concern about role
adjustment (e.g., job morale). Those tests derived from a
more individual psychodynamic orientation contain factors
related to emotional control and somatic distress that are of
less interest to sociologists. The convergence here, I
believe, is more important than the differences. Further
work will no doubt clarify the overlaps and differences.

I would like to mention one methodological constant,
that is the reliance on self-report. Some critics of
attempts to develop measures of psychological well-being have
been disturbed by the fact that we must rely on self-reports.
How nice it would be if we could detect brain waves or chemi-
cal substances in the blood that would be good indicators of
overall well-being! If we could read data as output from an
electronic instrument, how much more objective and scientific
it would be! Or perhaps we should not rely on self-report,
but on the observations of individuals' behavior by other
people--friends, family members, or trained observers.
Observational methods have been tried in smaller studies,
sometimes with considerable ingenuity and effort, but the
results to date seem even less promising than those based on
self-report.

Are we seriously mistaken in our reliance on self-
report? Is it only a second best accommodation to the expense and difficulty of other methods? I think not. There
is something intrinsic to the phenomenon of psychological
well-being that makes self-report the appropriate method.
After all, it is the thoughts and feelings of individuals
that make up what we call psychological well-being. There
may be troublesome situations in which people are motivated
to report their experiences falsely, a situation that was
worrisome to the authors of The American Soldier. One can
take steps to try to screen out such cases where there is
reason to believe that false reporting will be going on. But

for the general purposes of measuring well-being that we have been talking about, there do not seen to me to be any greater problems in response bias than there are with any other kind of self-report measure, including reports of physical symptoms that are important to the assessment of physical health.

I have reviewed briefly the development of measures of psychological well-being from the beginnings during the Second World War down to the current efforts at NCHS to establish a measure of general usefulness as part of our national health statistical programs. I believe that similar attempts are underway in other countries, notably in the Canadian Health Survey. I hope that these efforts are at least to some extent co-ordinated so that we can have measures as comparable as possible across countries.

In this review I have noted the evolution of the methodology from a questionnaire used as a screening device to reduce the number of individuals interviewed by psychiatrists; to structured interview schedules administered by professionally trained social scientists used as proxies for psychiatric interviews, but with the ratings still being done by psychiatrists; to largely pre-coded interview schedules administered by professional interviewers not specifically trained in social sciences; to completely pre-coded questionnaires capable of being self-administered (as were the original screening devices if one likes to think that we have come full circle). As the interview schedules become more standardized and pre-coded, the data are treated more quantitatively, and the psychiatrists as independent raters drop by the wayside. Ultimately the questionnaires yield their own quantitative scores that become the measures of interest.

While the methods have evolved, the content has stayed relatively constant. I have already noted that the broad content areas of current functioning that were in the original screening device--sociability, worry, sensitivity, personal adjustment and somatic complaints--have survived in one form or another as a major part of the interviews. But these areas are very general and not altogether separate. Thus while there is a general consensus about the importance of such content areas, there is no agreement yet about the specific areas nor indeed how many separate areas there are.

The problem is analogous to that in intelligence testing where there has been long debate about a single general factor of intelligence versus several specific factors. The failure to resolve that debate fully, however, has not

prevented the development and widespread use of intelligence
measures. It need not prevent the employment of measures of
psychological well-being. I am optimistic that by the end of
a decade, we will have an instrument for measuring general
well-being that will be administered on a periodic basis to
samples of the U.S. population, and that we shall begin to
have more solid knowledge about the mental health of the
population.

References and Notes

1. I thank Carrie Miles for help in the preparation of this paper.
2. S. A. Stouffer, L. Guttman, E. A. Suchman, P. F. Lazarsfeld, S. A. Star and J. A. Clausen, Studies in Social Psychology in World War II: Vol. 4. Measurement and Prediction (Princeton University Press, Princeton, N.J., 1950.
3. D. C. Leighton, J. S. Harding, O. B. Macklin, A. M. MacMillan and A. H. Leighton, The Character of Danger (Basic Books, New York, 1963).
4. L. Srole, T. S. Langner, S. T. Michael, M. K. Opler and T. A. C. Rennie, Mental Health in the Metropolis: The Mid-town Manhatten Study (McGraw-Hill, New York, 1962).
5. G. Gurin, J. Veroff and S. Feld, Americans View Their Mental Health (Basic Books, New York, 1960).
6. N. M. Bradburn and D. Caplovitz, Reports on Happiness: A Pilot Study of Behavior Related to Mental Health (Aldine, Chicago, 1965).
7. N. M. Bradburn, The Structure of Psychological Well-being (Aldine, Chicago, 1969).
8. H. J. Dupuy, "Developmental Rationale, Substantive, Derivative, and Conceptual Relevance of the General Well-being Schedule" (Unpublished working paper, 1973).
9. K. Schuessler and L. Freshnock, "Measuring Attitudes Toward Self and Others in Society: State of the Art" (Unpublished paper, Dept. of Sociology, University of Indiana, 1976).

7

Measurement of Oral Health Status

Mata K. Nikias

Introduction

The characteristics of oral health problems and of their
treatment are the primary factors which have determined the
characteristics of oral health status indicators and the
special potential for measurement in the field of oral health.
Oral health assessments are possibly more objective, repro-
ducible and quantifiable compared to those in other health
fields. Thus oral health status indexes are especially useful for the formulation of policy and detailed planning for
oral health.

The most common diseases of the mouth (dental caries
and periodontal disease) are almost universal in prevalence;
their attack is continuously recurring; they do not undergo
remission or termination if untreated, but accumulate a back-
log of need for dental treatment. If left untreated, they
both lead to tooth loss. On the other hand much of dental
treatment results in permanent and early observable changes
in the appearance of the oral tissues.

In addition to being able to reflect dentistry's intervention, oral health status can also reflect to some extent
the person's behavior regarding his or her oral health. For
example, conscientious performance of certain oral hygiene
routines (brushing, flossing, mouth rinsing, diet modifications) will lead to changes of the hard and soft tissue (e.g.,
changes in amount of plaque and debris, calculus and gingival
inflammation) which are observable and measurable. Thus even
at their simplest level most of the oral status indicators
belong to the category of sociomedical indicators to the extent that they are measures not only of biologic aspects of
dental diseases but also of social behavioral factors related to the individual's and to the professional's attitudes
and actions for the prevention, neglect, control, and

management of oral diseases. Such sociomedical dimensions
have direct implications for the development of policy regarding oral health.

Other problems of oral health in addition to caries and
periodontal diseases, include two major categories of disease
entities: 1) oral-facial malformations and malocclusions;
and 2) soft tissue lesions including oral cancer. Malocclusions constitute a significant clinical problem but concern
primarily children. Cohen and Jago (1) have recently provided the most comprehensive review of measures of oral conditions and oral status outcomes as they are used in the
formulation of sociodental indicators.

While the detection of oral cancer and the control of
infection have a high priority in the management of oral
problems, dental caries and periodontal diseases will be the
major areas of concern in this paper. This emphasis is made
because these two oral health problems and their sequallae
account for the major suffering, tooth loss, and commitment
of dental resources in the private and public sectors. Even
restricting concern to the two main disease entities and to
the consequences of their treatment or lack of treatment,
their varying levels of prevalence and severity result in
very diverse quantitative and qualitative patterns of oral
conditions.

Thus indices which are currently in use or under development for the measurement of oral health status represent a
mixed spectrum of approaches in kind and number of oral clinical dimensions included in the components of the index,
measures of dental treatment, and of met and unmet needs for
dental care. It appears that numerous oral status indicators
were developed in order to serve the purposes of various scientific, research and professional perspectives and interest
groups. All of these indices are based on data obtained from
dental examinations and all have elements of usefulness for
the policy maker and/or the planner.

For the purposes of the present discussion a dual classification of oral health indices is made by indicator type
and by indicator purpose: 1) Specific Dental Disease Indices; 2) Multidimensional Oral Health Status Indices, or
Profiles; and 3) Indices of Dental Needs. The above classification scheme is roughly paralleled by another, reflecting
respectively the different purposes, and perspectives that
had to be served by the three categories of indices. The
second classification includes: 1) Clinical and Epidemiologic studies, 2) Assessment of Oral Health Levels of Populations and Sociodental Research, 3) Planning and Evaluations

of Oral Health Care. The classification of indicators is
not mutually exclusive and one group of indices may be applicable to more than one perspective or purpose, yet the distinction is still valid when one considers the primary
function and the best fit.

This paper describes the current state of the art in
approaches to measurement of oral health along the lines of
these two parallel classifications, that is of the indices
and of their purposes.

Specific Dental Disease Indices
(Clinical and Epidemiologic Perspectives)

These are the traditional indices that developed to
serve the needs for clinical and epidemiologic studies, primarily of caries and periodontal diseases. Clinical studies
are intended primarily to assess the effectiveness of preventive and therapeutic measures, while epidemiologic surveys
are concerned with the prevalence and distribution of the
disease in population groups. Properties that such indices
should have include the following: 1) the index must be
simple and quick to use and permit the study of large numbers
of persons, 2) guidelines defining the components of the index should be clear and understandable to promote accuracy
and reproducibility, 3) the index should quantify severity
of the disease with equal sensitivity throughout the clinical stages of the disease process, 4) the index should be
amenable to statistical analysis (2).

Epidemiologic data on the incidence and prevalence of
dental diseases, which are highly quantifiable, provide
planners with a descriptive data base which is used to quantify with considerable precision the extent and distribution
of specific dental problems in target populations. Having
done this, the first policy issue concerns how to bring dental treatment to those who need it most. This can be effec-
ted by consumer education to induce effective demand for
dentists' services or by increased availability and accessibility and reduced cost of dental services. At another level
information on prevalence of dental disease can be readily
translated into quantitative measures of needs for dental
services and to a certain degree into professional human
power, time, and costs estimates which are important for
planning and for decisions on resource allocation.

Dental Caries

Assessments of dental caries illustrate the high level
of measurability and objectivity that can be achieved in the

dental field. A variety of measures of caries experience
has been suggested using the person, the tooth, the surface
of the tooth or the carious lesion as the basis of measurement. The most highly developed and widely accepted, however, is the DMF index (D=Decayed, M=Missing and F=Filled
teeth). The DMF index has been extended to describe caries
experience also on tooth surfaces (DMFS). It is arrived at
by making discrete counts of DMF teeth or surfaces after a
simple mouth examination. For example, recent data from
adults enrolled in a group practice medical plan in New York
City showed that the mean number of missing and unreplaced
teeth in the poverty group was 9.6 and in the nonpoverty
group 7.0. The mean number of decayed teeth was 1.6 for
poverty and 1.0 for nonpoverty and the mean number of filled
teeth was 5.3 for poverty and 9.1 for nonpoverty group (3).
Obviously such data have direct implications for policy decisions and program planning to control dental caries in
varied socioeconomic population groups. Targeted groups of
this nature would be Medicaid and welfare beneficiaries.

The DMF index is a fairly reliable measure of dental
caries experience among children and young persons. However since teeth may be missing for reasons other than
caries it is less reliable among older adults. To overcome
such limitations ratios made up of components of the DMF
have also been proposed and used such as D/DMF, or DM/DMF or
of those of decayed teeth over the total number of teeth
present in the mouth (4).

Periodontal Disease

Periodontal disease is a disease of the tissues sup-
porting the teeth. The inflammatory process involves only
the gums or gingivae (gingivitis). However, if unchecked
there is detachment of the periodontal fibers, formation of
pockets, loss of bone, and the tooth becomes loose, extruded
and lost.

The nature of periodontal disease, precludes accurate
measures of current disease, past disease and past treatment
that we have in dental caries through the DMF. The revers-
ible nature of gingivitis following treatment can lead to
underestimation of previous treatment. While a treatment
procedure like gingivectomy would constitute a more tangible
evidence of previous periodontal therapy, it is much less
observable and therefore less quantifiable than a filling
material in the treatment for dental caries.

Objective measurement of periodontal disease itself is
also far more difficult than the objective measurement of

caries. There is greater subjectivity and inter- and intra-
examiner variability in the diagnoses and evaluations of different aspects of periodontal problems. Within the past 25
years numerous indices have been devised and used to measure
the presence and severity of periodontal disease. The existence of numerous indices highlights the fact that there is
no one comprehensive, widely acceptable index to satisfy all
purposes and all investigators. Illustrative is the work of
a special task force which recently distinguished among indices for measuring different aspects of periodontal disease:
1) soft accumulations, 2) hard deposits, 3) gingival inflammation, 4) loss of periodontium, and 5) tooth mobility (5).

   In addition to the above indices which measure a single
component or process of periodontal disease, there are periodontal indices that combine the processes associated with
periodontal disease. Among these composite indices the most
widely acceptable and used for epidemiologic studies is
Russell's Index (6). The Russell Index includes components
of gingival inflammation, pocket formation, bone loss and
tooth mobility. Another composite index is Ramfjord's P.D.I.
Index (7) which combines measures of calculus with pocket
depth and other components. Because of the universal distribution of gingival and periodontal problems all types of
indices include some measure of severity. These form ordinal
scales or ranks with a higher score implying a greater severity.

   Oral Hygiene Indices - are also composite measures
quantifying clinical components involved in periodontal problems but in addition have been used to provide a measure of
patients' oral hygiene practices (8,9). By recording degrees of stain, debris, and calculus they summarize oral
hygiene status and may be used as a measure of dental neglect
as well as current or past personal oral hygiene behavior.
These indices are used for measuring the effectiveness of
health education programs in improving the oral health of
the population through instituting recommended home practices and behavior change rather than through receipt of
professional services. Such assessments have implications
for policy decisions and allocation of resources to large
scale public health education programs aiming at individual
behavior change.

   Besides providing disease prevalence data, the groups
of specific dental disease indices are useful to the health
planner because they furnish research data on the effectiveness of certain preventive and therapeutic interventions.
In the planning process the effect of their application on
the health status of the individuals on whom they would be

applied can be estimated. These estimates together with
disease prevalence data in the reference population can
provide   cost benefit assessments of particular forms of
intervention. At the policy level the most effective,
efficient and acceptable strategy can be recommended for
large scale implementation.

Indices of Other Oral Conditions

Very few other specific oral indices have been developed beyond those discussed regarding dental caries and
periodontal diseases. Malocclusions form a special category
of conditions. However their measurement efforts are not
included in the present discussion covered here. They are
the most difficult of oral conditions to measure - not the
least because there are no clear definitions of what constitutes "malocclusion." A comprehensive review of the
state of the art in the measurement and epidemiology of
malocclusions using the findings of 44 studies in 18 countries has been recently provided by Jago (10) who highlights
the attempts and difficulties involved in the search for an
absolute objective index of malocclusion. Emphasis is
directed at one which would incorporate social psychological
as well as clinical criteria.

Multidimensional Oral Status Indices or Profiles
(Assessment of The Level of Overall Oral Health
and Sociodental Research Perspectives)

So far,we have considered a sampling from categories of
indices each summarizing a distinct oral condition. The
DMF index measures caries; several indices have been devised to assess periodontal disease, malocclusions, oral
hygiene status, and oral hygiene practices. However, each
of these measures used separately do not provide a reasonably accurate picture of the status of total oral health.
For example, looked at in terms of caries alone, a decay
free mouth may be termed healthy while gross periodontal
disease is present and many teeth are already lost. Con-
versely, many teeth with active caries may exist in a
healthy periodontium with varying levels of oral hygiene and
tooth loss. Some of the questions asked when considering
the development of appropriate oral health indices are: do
certain conditions tend to occur singly or in combination
with others? How can it be determined which combinations of
condition represent a healthier mouth than another?

A comprehensive measure of oral health should depict
all the multiple disease processes acting in the mouth and
their effects: incorporating also subjective aspects of

pain, function, esthetics, well-being and other psychological and social behavioral dimensions. However even restricting concern to the clinical domain, compilation of a
comprehensive index appears to be a complex problem because
of the wide qualitative and quantitative range of conditions
occurring in the mouth.

The distinct advantage of a multidimensional oral
status index is that it enables us to summarize diverse elements into a single, meaningful concept expressed as a number. This in turn is useful in the assessment and comparison of oral health levels in subgroups of populations, as
well as populations of different countries, and in assessing
changes in oral health over time. A comprehensive index
also facilitates the work of sociodental researchers in
search of determinants of oral health status. The index
serves as an outcome variable in studies to elicit relationships among a multiplicity of demographic, socioeconomic,
cultural, and behavioral variables and oral health viewed
in a generic sense. This identification of determinants of
observed distributions of total oral health, as opposed to
only of specific diseases, has relevance to policy and resource allocation. It is one of the mandates of the local
Health Systems' Agencies as delineated in the National
Health Planning and Resources Development Act, P.L. 93-641.
There have been a few attempts to combine several oral clinical dimensions into a more general index of oral health.

National Dental Health Index in Canada

One such attempt is the National Dental Health Index
(NDHI) which has been in process of development by the
Canadian Dental Association since 1958 to study national
variation and trends in dental disease(s) (11). The index
provides comparative data for four classes: 1) relative
prevalence of dental caries, 2) relative prevalence of
periodontal disease, 3) relative prevalence of malocclusion,
4) relative degree of treatment accomplished. Although
criteria for definitions were developed and collection of
data accomplished for each of the components of the NDHI, so
far there has been no report of calculation of a Canadian
national dental health index from a dental health survey of
Canadian Provinces during 1968-1970 (12).

The Oral Health Grading in England

Another promising, although incomplete, attempt to combine various clinical aspects of oral health into one measure is the Oral Health Grading developed by Bulman et al. in
their sociodental study of two contrasting urban areas in

England (13). These investigators regarded the attempt as
"merely one step towards a satisfactory solution" to the
compilation of an index of oral health which will take into
account the condition of all oral tissues. Oral health here
was considered under three main components: dental, periodontal, and prosthetic and each component was divided in
three grade levels "good," "fair," and "poor." The researchers attested that more than three grades leads to confusion in definition and interpretation and less than three
to lack of adequate information. A six-digit code can thus
give a measure of any individual's oral status. After
eliminating or combining codes which occurred in only a
small number of people the codes were summarized in a seven
point ordinal scale so that any individual could be assigned
an oral health score between 1 and 7.

    The investigators have identified several limitations
to this first attempt to develop a composite oral health
index. One difficulty was how to deal with missing teeth
which are replaced and not replaced. Another limitation is
the fact that a poor grading on the first dimension (i.e.
dental) may refer to loss of all teeth or to gross decay on
all teeth. These two oral states are different both in
terms of prognosis as well as type and extent of treatment
needed. An additional problem is posed by the classes that
have very few people in them. The most important limitation
is the arbitrariness in assigning ranks and scores in the
different (3-divisional) categories . While the extreme
ends of the scale present no problem, between these limits
the order is liable to dispute.

    Apparently a major difficulty in the development of a
single composite index of oral health is establishing a
system for appropriately weighting the different oral status
dimensions relative to their contribution to total oral
health. Is the periodontal condition more important than
the condition of individual teeth or vice versa? Such
questions exist because of the difficulty of achieving consensus as to what constitutes better or worse states of
oral health. Depending on the primary evaluative dimension
used, different decisions can be made. The person's age,
prognosis, masticatory and speech functions, symptoms and
problems, esthetic and other social behavioral factors as
well as the judge's own values and opinions enter in making
such decisions. Thus devising a meaningful formula for
combining and weighting oral status dimensions for the com-
putation of a simple numerical index becomes a complex and
difficult process even when concern is narrowed to the
clinical level.

Multidimensional Oral Status
Profiles in New York City

The need however for some summarization of at least
the most common oral conditions continues to exist as well
as the need to find out and characterize the extent of professional consensus regarding definitions of oral health.
At present at Columbia University and at the Health Insurance Plan of Greater New York we are engaged in a research
project whose aims are first, the development of multidimensional clinical profiles of oral status and then, the
ranking of these profiles by panels of dental professionals
(14). This investigation will determine the feasibility of
developing a composite oral health index incorporating professional consensus and provides a starting point and some
empirical data for the development of a weighting system.
The four clinical dimensions used in the profile of oral
status are: 1) number of missing and unreplaced teeth,
2) levels of periodontal disease, 3) decayed teeth, and
4) oral hygiene status.

Four groups of selected dental professionals have been
asked to rank each of 42 four-dimensional profiles on a
nine-point scale ranging from "best"(1) to "worst"(9) oral
status. These four panels of judges themselves have been
classified according to their main professional perspective
and activity as: dental researchers, public health dentists, part-time academic or research dentists, and general
dental practitioners. Although analyses have just been
started, preliminary results show high intra- and inter-
panel agreement for profiles representing extreme states of
oral health. However, the middle range showed varying
amounts of disagreement both between and within panels of
judges. Deviations among intra- and inter- panel rankings
are being analyzed to arrive at an appropriate statistic to
represent the average rank for each profile. At a subsequent stage oral status as measured by a scale rather than
by a disease-categorical approach will be examined for its
relationship to various demographic and sociobehavioral
variables in the search for oral health correlates and
determinants.

Indices of Oral Health Needs
(Perspectives for Planning and
Evaluation of Oral Health Care)

So far, we have been discussing various indices of
oral status which, although they may change in relation to
provision of dental care, do not necessarily include indicators of the extent that past oral health needs of the

person have received appropriate care.

When assessing oral health for the purposes of determining the dental care, if any, needed to restore oral
health to optimum levels, indices of oral health needs are
relevant concepts and measures. Their measurability and
potential for quantification have direct practical utility
for effective planning of oral health care programs. At
the same time the extent and kind of met dental needs and
their relationships to unmet needs constitute meaningful
outcome measures for evaluating the effectiveness of both
dental care programs and the general success of given dental
care systems in improving levels of oral health. Such indices derived from population groups can give planners an
indication of long term effectiveness. The continuation,
change or interruption of the program can then be recommended.

In addition to assessments of the effectiveness of the
overall program, in dentistry – where much of the treatment
results in permanent changes in the appearance of the oral
tissues – there is an unusual opportunity to evaluate the
quality of treatment in numerous aspects. An example is
assessing the technical quality of treatment procedures such
as amalgam restorations or partial dentures. Many studies
of quality of care have already been conducted using the
latter approach. Data from clinical examination or from
review of records of patients who have received services
are compared against standards usually developed by academic
dentists. What is judged here is the "degree of goodness"
of the specific procedure. Evaluations based on the mix of
services received (e.g., preventive and restorative services
versus tooth extractions) as well as on the extent that all
necessary services are completed can also be made relatively
more objectively in dental care compared to other areas of
health care.

However, an index of dental need is not an index of
oral health and in fact sometimes the two may even be in-
versely related. For instance many feel that missing teeth
represent an irreversible failure to maintain optimum oral
health and therefore tooth loss should receive the greatest
negative weight in any consideration of oral health regardless of replacement status by prostheses. Thus a person
who wears full dentures would perhaps tend to fall in the
lowest end on a scale of oral health, but would be in the
opposite end on a scale of unmet needs.

Various approaches have been used and are being developed for measuring dental needs. Most of them were

specifically developed to meet the objectives of specific
research projects and of dental care delivery programs in
special study samples or target populations. In the following section we describe a sampling of illustrative, recent,
and promising efforts.

Specific Dental Disease
Treatment Needs

This category includes assessment of services needed
to treat specific dental diseases. Again, dental caries is
the oral disease for which we have the most precise and ver-
satile measurements. For example, DMF can be looked at,
sectioned according to its components with the D component
indicating the average number of teeth in need of treatment
for caries (unmet caries need) and F showing the mean number which have been filled for carious lesions (met caries
need). The M component however cannot be interpreted in
terms of need for caries treatment because the DMF index
does not differentiate between missing teeth which are unreplaced and those which are replaced with prostheses.
Furthermore, in adults DMF is not an effective measure of
caries because the cause for most missing teeth is periodontal disease. Thus more recently other indices are used to
measure treatment needs for caries.

For example a measure of unmet restorative treatment
needs (UTN) is the ratio of decayed teeth over those decayed plus filled. This index was used to measure and
compare the caries needs of male Puerto Rican Migrant
Workers in Massachusetts with that of all U.S. males as
determined from data of the National Health Survey (15).
It was found that the unmet restorative needs for all U.S.
males ranged from 13 to 22 percent, while the range for
migrants was 75 to 92 percent. Such ratios provide planners with a sound basis for the allocation of caries treatment resources and a logical basis for identifying population subgroups of high need for services. These ratios
also are a basis for assigning priorities and developing
special health care projects. For example in our studies
of adult enrollees at the Health Insurance Plan in New York
City, we assessed treatment needs for caries using the Decayed Teeth Ratio (4). This ratio was calculated by di-
viding the number of decayed teeth by the number of teeth
which were present in the mouth. The formula is as follows:

Decayed Teeth Ratio = $\frac{D}{D+F+S}$X 100   (where D=decayed teeth;
F=filled teeth; S=sound untreated teeth).

We found that the proportion of the Medicaid group who had
high levels of untreated decay (e.g., in more than one out
of five teeth) was three times greater than the study's
highest economic group. Meaningful measures of treatment
for caries (met caries needs) have also been used based on
components of the DMF. The Restorative Index (RI) suggested by Jackson (16) measures the proportion of attacked
teeth that have been filled by calculating the ratio of
filled teeth to those filled plus decayed ($[F/F+D]$ X 100)(16).
By applying this index on U.S. National Health Survey data
for the years 1960-1962 and on a North Carolina Survey data
in 1960, Jackson found that in both surveys the RI for the
black adult population was approximately half that found in
the white population. In our data of enrollees of the
Health Insurance Plan in New York City the index showed that
proportion of the Medicaid group who had RI 100 percent (all
their affected teeth restored) was half that of the study's
highest economic group (4).

It is far more difficult to quantify treatment needs
for periodontal disease than for caries. A noteworthy
effort is the Periodontal Treatment Need System (PTNS) recently developed and tested in Oslo, Norway (17,18). It
expresses periodontal needs in a classification according
to the type of periodontal treatment procedures and relates
them to time requirements: Class 0 - no clinical signs of
inflammation; Class A - individual motivation and instruction in oral hygiene. Class B - scaling and elimination of
overhangs; Class C - periodontal surgery. The average time
for the performance of the treatment types for each class
have been estimated as: Class A = 60 minutes per patient,
Class B = 30 minutes per mouth quadrant; Class C = 60
minutes per quadrant (17). The PTNS is an ordinal scale
with classes A, B, and C respectively indicating mild,
moderate, and severe periodontal disease states and is not
an index of need expressed numerically. However, it is
directly useful to planners because it establishes a basis
for calculation of human power and costs.

Multidimensional Dental
Need Measures

A first attempt to develop a comprehensive multidimensional Index of Dental Need (IDN) was that by Lambert,
Freeman, and their co-workers in a study of teenagers in
Boston (19). This index combined the number of decayed
teeth surfaces divided in three levels, periodontal conditions (measured by the gingival-bone count also in three
levels) and orthodontic rating divided into two categories

("need" and "no need" for orthodontic treatment). The IDN
was expressed not as a numerical value but on a nominal
three-point scale of low, medium and high. To be applicable to adults, an index of dental need should also provide
for the wider full range of oral conditions both common and
rare.

Other approaches to conceptualize and measure overall
dental needs have considered the dimensions of urgency and
severity of the presenting problem or problems rather than
the combination of clinical conditions. Urgency determines
the point in time that professional intervention is needed
and the degree of severity determines the amount of resources which will be required to restore oral health. Urgency can be expressed as the length of time specified types
of services can be deferred without risking further deterio-
ration of the patient's oral health status. Based on urgency, Schoen and Friedman developed a four-point classification scheme of a Dental Care Priority System: Class I:
Very Urgent - Functional and Social Disability (those conditions requiring rapid attention); Class II: Moderately
Urgent (those conditions requiring care in the near future);
Class III: Non-Urgent (those conditions requiring care, but
postponable for a period; Class IV: Maintenance (no special
conditions exist requiring remedial treatment), patients
placed on routine prophylaxis and recall care (20). These
classifications are proposed as a means for establishing
program priorities directly relevant to planning. According to Schoen and Friedman this classification helps manage
logically rapid influx of a large number of new patients to
a dental care delivery system with limited manpower and
financial support. It is also suggested as appropriate for
the care of individual patients based on a concept which
recognizes that many oral conditions are chronic and also
that some patients cannot or will not comply with treatment
recommendations.

Currently the Dental Care Systems Unit at the School of
Dental Medicine of the University of Pennsylvania is at-
tempting to develop an Index of Need for use in clinical
practice that takes into account both urgency and severity
of presenting oral health problems (21). This Index of Need
is thought of as a quantitative tool for assisting a dental
practice in properly managing both the urgency and severity
dimensions of oral health problems in the population for
which it is responsible. It utilizes numerical scales for
urgency and severity, each having only a few defined points.
Dental needs of any patient can be classified by the clini-
cian's determination of how presenting conditions relate to

the vectors of urgency and severity. The highest numerical
rating would be assigned to the highest category of need.
This index can be used for estimating the short and long
range demands on the dental care system, as well as for
evaluating the success of the system in improving levels of
oral health.

The concept and measures of unmet health needs are also
relevant and have been applied to dental needs. An Unmet
Dental Needs component has been incorporated in the comprehensive scales of the Meharry Medical College Study of Unmet Health Needs (22). An unmet need is defined as the absence of any, or of sufficient, or of appropriate care or
services. It is operationalized as the difference between
services judged necessary to deal appropriately with health
problems and services actually received. As such they indicate the extent to which medical and dental knowledge is
being applied in the population groups studied. Judgments
about unmet dental needs are made by a dentist based on
several specific disease indices which are calculated from
clinical examination recordings. These indices include a
Caries Conduciveness Test, the Oral Hygiene Index Simplified, the Handicapping-Labio-Lingual Deviations Index as a
measure of occlusion, Russell's Periodontal Index as well
as DMF scores. Based on the findings from a mouth examination, and history and information about dental care received, an overall judgment about unmet need is made by the
dentist. Ratings are assigned on a five-point scale ranging
from 0 (none) to 5 (great) (23). So far unmet dental needs
in this study are expressed in an ordinal scale based only
on professional judgment. However, the potential and the
required data on the specific dental disease indices exist
for developing a methodology which will weigh and combine
the various dental indicators and lead to an objective
quantitative index of unmet needs for dental care directly
useful for planning and evaluation.

Since it is possible for the prevalence of disease and
unmet needs to vary independently from the provision of
care, another meaningful approach for evaluating the effectiveness of the health system is to look at the opposite
side of the coin, namely at a measure of needs which have
been met through the provision of appropriate care. The
ratio of services provided in relation to needed services
S/N constitutes a valid operational index for this purpose.
This approach has been advanced and put to practical application by a unique research project in the dental field,
the World Health Organization/Division of Dentistry International Collaborative Study of Dental Manpower Systems (24).

The objective of this ambitious study is to examine the relationship between structural features of national dental care delivery systems and oral status outcomes and needs in the population. For such international comparisons of system components, the measure for the dependent or outcome variable should reflect the extent that dental services provided in a given country fill the dental needs of the people in that country irrespective of the country's overall level of oral health, since baseline oral status levels and disease patterns among countries or societies can vary for factors unrelated to the dental delivery system. Such factors include genetic characteristics leading to greater susceptibility or resistance to dental disease, natural fluoride in the area, nutritional patterns, etc. Using ratios of services over need circumvents the influence of geographical and cultural factors. It thus reduces the risk of faulty international comparisons because of pre-existing differences in disease prevalence not necessarily system-related or because of inter-system differences in the definitions of dental needs and in employed treatment modalities.

In initial analyses of the international study treatment/need ratios have been applied on DMF data in order to assess differences in meeting the need for treatment of caries irrespective of the prevalence of dental caries (25). The approach is illustrated by the way with which missing teeth (M) are dealt. A missing tooth for which replacement is needed but not provided enters the need part of the ratio only, whereas a missing tooth which has been replaced by a prosthesis is included in both treatment and need totals. If the replacement needs to be redone, that tooth is included in both retreatment and need totals and if a missing tooth is judged to need no replacement it does not figure in the ratio. Additional useful concepts and measures used in calculating ratios in this study relate to retreatment needs (e.g., teeth already filled but needing further treatment because of recurrent caries or faulty restorations) for which there is little or no previous epidemiologic data. Concepts and measures of retreatment needs are useful not only for evaluating quality of dental services but also for gaining an understanding of the function of, and need for the periodicity of patient recall visits in dental care facilities.

Assessment of requirements for prosthetic treatment was also made for adults in this study by classifying the population samples (separately for dentures and bridges) under the following categories: have no dentures or bridges need none; have none need some; have some need none; have

some need some. These categories indicate respectively
treatment never needed, unmet need, met need, and partly
met need.

This international project is still at its first stage
of data analysis, and the potential of the usefulness of the
approach has not been fully realized. However the protocol
allows for sets of statistics to measure several parameters
which may permit a deeper understanding not only of oral
health components but also of factors that influence them.

Conclusions

This review indicates that a wide spectrum of different
types of oral status indicators have been developed and are
used to serve the purposes of different scientific and professional perspectives and interest groups. These indicators can be used by the planners or policy makers in order
to do more educated planning and make more educated policy
decisions. Furthermore due to their relatively high quanti-
fiability and precision oral status data that are currently
available or collected routinely in the operation of various
dental care programs lend themselves readily to development
of indices with particular emphasis on their use in planning
and policy formulation. Remaining difficulties include the
complexity in meaningfully summarizing and weighing the
various conditions that occur in the mouth and the lack of
effort to incorporate social psychological components in
oral health indicators. Dimensions which need further research to determine their potential for being integrated in
a comprehensive oral health index are those reflecting the
impact of oral health on the quality of life. These are
factors such as disability, days lost from school or work
due to oral conditions, discomfort while at school or work
as a result of oral conditions, impact on appearance, and
relationship of appearance to constructive social interaction,and even the cost of dental treatment as a proportion
of the national health bill. The oral health field, however, provides unusual potential for increasing the ability
of sociomedical sciences to measure health status because it
has higher measurability relative to other health fields and
it reflects more readily the health behaviors of the individual, and of the professional as well as the practices,
policies, and goals of the dental care delivery system.

Acknowledgements

My thanks to Athilia E. Siegmann for helpful comments on this paper, Norma Agatstein and Lois K. Cohen for helpful comments on earlier versions, and Nancy Queen for excellent preparation of all typed copies.

References

1. L.K. Cohen, and J.D. Jago, Int. J. Health Serv. 6, 681 (1976).

2. P. Gjermo, J. Periodont. Res. 9, Suppl. 14, 70 (1974).

3. M.K. Nikias, R. Fink, and S. Shapiro, J. Public Health Dent. 35, 237 (1975).

4. M.K. Nikias, R. Fink and W. A. Sollecito, Community Dent. Oral Epidemiol. 5 (1977) (In press).

5. International Conference on Clinical Trials of Agents used in the Prevention/Treatment of Periodontal Diseases, J. Periodont. Res. 9 Suppl. 14 (1974).

6. A.L. Russell, J. Dent. Res. 35, 350 (1956).

7. S.P. Ramfjord, J. Periodont. 38, 602 (1967).

8. J.C. Greene and J.R. Vermillion, J. Am. Dent. Assoc. 68, 7 (1964).

9. A.G. Podshadley and J.V. Haley, Public Health Rep. 83, 259 (1968).

10. J.D. Jago, J. Public Health Dent. 34, 80 (1974).

11. The Evaluation of Canadian Dental Health – A System for Recording and Statistical Analysis at the Community, Provincial and National Level. Canadian Dental Association, Public Health Committee and Research Committee, Toronto, July 1959.

12. Dental Health Survey of Canadian Provinces 1968-1970. Results of a Field Trial of a Survey Method. Published by Authority of the Honorable Marc Lalonde, Minister of National Health and Welfare, Ottawa, 1973.

13. J.W. Bulman and N.D. Richards, Demand and Need for Dental Care: a Sociodental Study. (Nuffield Provincial Hospital Trust, Oxford University Press, London, England, 1968), pp. 97-103.

14. M.K. Nikias, W.A. Sollecito, and R. Fink, Oral status profiles in developing an oral health index. Paper presented at the 54th General Session of the International Association of Dental Research, Miami, Florida, March 1976.

15. G.M. Gluck , C.D. Knox, R.L. Glass, and M. Wolfman, Health Serv. Rep. 87, 456 (1972).

16. D. Jackson, Br. Dent. J. 134, 385 (1973).

17. H.T. Bellini and P. Gjermo, Community Dent. Oral Epidemiol. 1, 22 (1973).

18. J.R. Johansen, Estimation of periodontal treatment needs. (University of Oslo, Norway, 1976).

19. C. Lambert, Jr., and H.E. Freedman with J.M. Dunning, H.M. Hughes, E.C. Maloof, R. Morris, and L.J. Taubenhaus. The Clinic Habit (College and University Press, New Haven, Conn. 1967) pp. 45-53.

20. J.W. Friedman, in Group Practice and the Future of Dental Care, C.R. Jerge, W.E. Marshall, M.H. Schoen and J.W. Friedman, Eds. (Lea and Febiger, Philadelphia, 1974), pp. 160-179.

21. C.R. Jerge and R.M. Orlowski, Index of dental need. (University of Pennsylvania School of Dental Medicine, Dental Care Systems, 1976. Working paper.

22. W. Carr, and S. Wolfe, Int. J. Health Serv. 6, 417 (1976).

23. W. Carr and S. Wolfe, Unmet needs for dental services (Center for Health Care Research, Meharry Medical College, 1975) Working paper.

24. L.K. Cohen and D.E. Barmes, Social Science and Medicine 8, 325 (1974).

25. D.E. Barnes, Progress report of the WHO/USPHS international collaborative study. Paper delivered at the 64th Annual Meeting of the Federation Dentaire Internationale, Athens, Greece, September 1976. Forthcoming in the International Dental Journal.

8

Methodological Perspectives on Health Status Indexes

Thomas W. Bice and Mary Jane Budenstein

Introduction

Enactment of the National Health Planning and Resources Development Act of 1974 has stimulated renewed and more focused attention on the need for information on which to base resource allocation decisions. Central to the purposes and processes of health planning defined in the Act is the measurement of the health status of populations in terms of its implications for needs for services, their effectiveness, and costs. These intended purposes, along with other more conventional criteria, provide a basis upon which to assess the relative merits of the plethora of health status indexes[1] proposed in the literature.

In this paper we identify the types of health status indexes required for health planning and describe various methodological approaches employed to date to deal with two fundamental problems of measurement, namely, concept specification and scaling of indicators[2].

Uses of Health Status Data
in Health Planning

Health planning involves several interrelated steps, each of which requires information about health status[3]. The process begins with a recognition of problems and a statement of goals or objectives. At this stage, situational analysis concentrates on describing a problem and its characteristics and magnitude in relation to a statement of objectives expressed in terms of desired directions and magnitudes of changes. Epidemiological data on the incidence and prevalence of health problems provides the descriptive

base needed to quantify the extent of the problem in the
reference population.

Such information combined with knowledge of the relative
efficacy of various potential modes of intervention trans-
lates the problem into quantitative expressions of needs for
services. A recent World Health Organization report on
health planning defined efficacy as "the benefit or utility
to the individual of the service, treatment regimen, drug,
preventive or control measure advocated or applied"(4).
Research on the efficacy of interventions provides the planner with transition probabilities which measure the likelihood that their application will effect changes in the
health status of individuals to whom they are applied. These
probabilities applied to the prevalence of problems in the
reference population yield a schedule of estimates of needs
for particular forms of intervention and projections of
their probable impacts.

The selection of implementation plans from available
alternative technologies involves a balancing of benefits
in relation to costs that requires health status indexes
expressed in terms of amounts and types of resources needed
to attain stated goals. Assuming that efficacious interventions exist, attention is directed toward determining
which processes and structures are the most effective,
efficient, and acceptable means of making them available
to the population.

Criteria for Evaluating Health Status Indexes

These various uses of information about health in the
planning process impose several demands on health status
indexes which can be employed as criteria in evaluating
them. Basically, these criteria do not differ from conventional standards of measurement applied in all scientific
research, which focus on concept specification--the means
by which abstract constructs are translated into operational
language and indicators--and scaling procedures--the means
by which numerals are assigned objects or events(5).
Ordinarily, these problems are somewhat simplified in
discipline-oriented research by the existence of theoretical
frames of reference that direct researchers' attention to
particular aspects of phenomena when specifying concepts
and by supplying conventional metric units in which to express measurements. In applied research where typically
neither set of rules exists, the investigator must choose
from among several plausible approaches.

Applying these conventional standards in combination with the practical needs of health planning, we identify four fundamental criteria for evaluating health status indexes. The first two pertain to the problem of concept specification, the third to scaling, and the fourth to practical problems of implementation and feasibility.

1. An index should provide a rationale for its selection of underlying dimensions. Several authors have observed that, since the concept of health is inherently multidimensional, no single index can capture all that the term implies. In consequence, measurement of health status requires conscious and systematic selection from several plausible aspects of what is conventionally meant by "health" the dimension (or dimensions) to be reflected in a particular index. Sullivan notes that most conceptions of health status are based on some combination of clinical, subjective, and behavioral dimensions(6).

2. An index should be sufficiently sensitive to detect significant changes in health status and be comprehensive enough to include a full range of events and circumstances experienced by the reference population. These criteria are, of course, mutually conflicting, for greater specificity is often gained at the expense of wider generality, and vice versa. The choice of which to maximize should be made in light of the purposes of the proposed index.

3. An index should be weighted by some metric which is relevant to one or more of the uses of health status indexes in the planning process. As we shall see, several indexes are expressed in convenient but arbitrary units while others assign weights to health status in terms of their implied needs for care, their relative utilities to people, and other dimensions of normative interest.

4. Finally, an index should be comprised of data that can be readily obtained, summarized, and applied by potential users. This is a rather obvious and therefore somewhat difficult criterion to operationalize, and, as Bush and his associates have cautioned, it should not be overstated(7). Ultimately, the cost and effort required by an index should be judged by its informative value in decision making.

Types of Health Status Indexes

The sheer number and diversity of health status indicators in the literature precludes an exhaustive survey of their relative merits. Moreover, as indexes are often proposed for application to specific diseases, to particular segments of the population, and to special settings or circumstances, we rarely find pairs of indexes that are directly comparable. Therefore, in this section we describe several illustrative approaches, applying our criteria to assess their strengths and weaknesses.

Health status indexes may be distinguished by three characteristics:

1. Their units of analysis
    a. Population aggregates
    b. Individuals

2. Their underlying dimensions, by which stages or categories are defined
    a. Clinical
    b. Subjective
    c. Behavioral

3. Their metric units

Together these determine the purposes for which they can be employed in health planning.

Population Aggregate Indexes

The earliest attempts to construct health status indexes were based on aggregate population rates of mortality and morbidity, the latter expressed in days of activity restriction. The indexes, scaled in terms of "days lost" are proposed as measures of the relative health of populations. Chiang's H(8), Sullivan's measure of "life free of disability"(9), and Chen's various formulations of the G index(10) illustrate various approaches taken to solve the problem of how to express in a single index the mortality and morbidity experience of populations.

Chiang proposed to measure the health of a population by the following formula:

$$H = 1 - \sum_x \overline{N}_x \overline{T}_x - \tfrac{1}{2}(m_x), \text{ where}$$

H = the portion of a year in which people are alive and free of disability

$\overline{N}_x$ = the average number of illnesses per person in age group x per year

$\overline{T}_x$ = the average duration of an illness for persons in age group x

m_x = age-specific death rate for the year

The index is based on data readily available for the nation as a whole, is relatively simple to compute, and is comprehensive. However, it is insensitive to differences in health status in that it distinguishes among only three states---death, alive with activity restriction, and alive with no activity limitation---and makes no distinctions among different levels of disability. Finally, the index is expressed in a convenient but uninterpretable metric of days lost (to death and disability) that is not related to any framework for evaluation, needs for services, or resource allocation.

Sullivan's approach to measuring the "expectation of life free of disability" is an improvement over Chiang's index in that it deals with the problem of how to combine mortality and morbidity over time. He proceeds by deducting age-specific fractions of years lost to disability from the standard life table, which yields a life expectancy free from disability and an expectation of life-time disability. The measure is easily computed from available national data. Like Chiang's index, however, it lacks sensitivity and is not scaled in terms of units directly relevant to the applied purposes of planning.

Chen's various formulations of the G index are proposed as means for establishing program priorities. He defines the total years lost to a target population due to a specific disease as the sum of fractions of years devoted to seeking medical attention and the mortality rate times the average number of years of life remaining for the total target population at the average age of death due to the disease. Identical computations are made for a reference population, from which expected values are derived for the target population. In turn, the sum of the expected days lost to mortality (D_1) and days lost to disability (D_2) is weighted by the ratio of the crude disease-specific mortality rate for the target population to that of the reference population. So constructed, Chen's indexes like Chiang's and Sullivan's, do not directly confront the issue of how to weight differentially years lost to death and years lost to disability. Furthermore, as the G index is proposed for use in disease-specific comparisions, it lacks generality and,

owing to the vast numbers of diseases afflicting populations,
it is unlikely that it could be used efficiently for its
intended purpose of establishing priorities.

A second approach to measuring the health of population
aggregates involves the use of factor analysis to summarize
the correlational structure among several indicators
Levine and Yett note that this method has several advantages,
including"...its ability to generate nonarbitrary, statisti-
cally verifiable groupings of related measures in the absence
of a priori theory, the ease with which various clusters may
be converted into composite indexes, and the fact that the
resulting groupings will closely reflect covariation in the
community's health status and its needs for health services"
(11).

As a practical matter, Levine and Yett are correct in
their recommending the factor analytic approach for summarizing vast numbers of indicators available from data reported
by the census. However, the very fact that the method requires no a priori theory detracts from their claim that resulting groupings will reflect a community's needs for health
services. In their application of factor analysis to New
Haven census tracts they found four interpretable factors,
one of which included (among other indicators) the percen-
tage of persons reporting health problems and a "low-rent
index." While these and other social indicators are readily
summarized by factor scores, their meanings in terms of needs
for services and resource allocations are not clear.

Clinically-Based Indexes

Most attempts to devise health status indexes based on
clinical data have been confined to single diseases and,
therefore, lack generality(12). An exception is Chen's -H
index, which he offers as a measure "primarily intended to
be applicable to individuals and groups or communities in
the premorbidity state"(13).

Conceiving of health status as an aggregate of numerous
physiological dimensions, Chen proposes to measure health
status by a weighted sum of an individual's deviations from
"ideal norms." Blood pressures, pulse rates, and other such
measures are transformed to standard scores, weighted by
expert opinion as to their seriousness, and summed. The
resulting -H index is proposed for use in evaluating intervention programs and as a prognostic tool.

While Chen's approach is logically and intuitively
appealing in its linking health status directly to

physiological and other clinical functions, its application is fraught with difficulties. It provides no basis for the selection of indicators from the vast array of potentially available clinical data and is weighted only in terms of medically-defined seriousness. Presumably, other weighting schemes based on needs for care could be devised. However, the likely expense of generating such weights and of collecting clinical data would be prohibitive.

Functional Status Indexes

Most health status indexes in recent literature are based on conceptions of functional status. Typically, several ordinal states are defined along an underlying functional status dimension ranging from total disability to well-being. Such indexes differ in terms of their specificity and the degree to which they distinguish among levels of "wellness," but all are reasonably comprehensive. However, most do not provide weights by which distances among various states can be given quantitative meaning. Two exceptions are the Health Status Index proposed by Bush and his colleagues(14) and the Sickness Impact Profile developed by Bergner and her associates(15).

The Health Status Index is a general formulation that takes into account operationally defined social preferences for function levels and expected transitions among levels over time. Therefore, the Index may be used not only to measure static health levels of populations but as well to project into the future impacts of intervention programs. The health of a population(H) is defined as:

$$H = E(F) = \sum_{j=1} F_j Y_j / Y, \text{ where}$$

H = health status of a population

$E(F)$ = the expected function level value over a "standard life" (100 Years)

F_j = social preference weight assigned to health state j

Y_j = expected total duration of function level j over all time periods

$Y = \sum_{j=1} y_j$ = total life expectancy

In our judgment, this index is the most promising general approach yet devised. Its conceptualization of the "standard life" and socially weighted function levels

provide a means of combining mortality and morbidity data in
a single index without equating time lost to death with time
lost to illness. Further, its explicit recognition of prog-
noses makes it a promising tool for program evaluation and
resource allocation.

The Sickness Impact Profile developed by Bergner and
her associates is intended for use in evaluating health
care programs. Based on an extensive study of patient-
reported daily life activities, the index is comprehensive,
and, due to its numerous dimensions, is likely to be sensitive to significant changes in functional status. Weights
developed by successive-interval methods appear to be
stable, and work is currently underway to develop a short
form version suitable for use in population surveys.

Conclusions

Although we have not attempted an exhasutive review of
the universe of health status indexes nor a detailed examination of each index we discussed, our review of the literature revealed some promising trends. In an earlier paper
the senior author noted what he regarded as a rather aim-
less development of indexes and unnecessary despair over
their inherent limitations(16). In the interim scholars
and practitioners have produced numerous indexes, which, in
our opinion, attempt to deal more explicitly with the potential uses of health status indexes. This is evidenced by
greater emphasis on both the conceptual and practical bases
of proposed measures and the problem of weighting health
state by application of various methods of measuring individuals' social preferences.

Especially encouraging in our opinion is current emphasis accorded the scaling problem. While in each instance,
one might reasonably argue with particular means employed to
give quantitative meaning to units along a continuum of
health or illness, at least the problem is being openly and
explicity debated. Such debate will undoubtedly call attention to some of the difficult value-laden decisions that are
implicit in planning under the assumptions of scarcity of
resources and competing values.

In this vein, we would observe that much of the public
clamor about health care costs and many reactive proposals
to control them lose sight of the real---though limited---
value of health care services. In so doing, we risk falling
prey to the cynicism, in Oscar Wilde's words, of knowing
the costs of everything and the value of nothing. Hopefully,
continued efforts to devise health status indexes will

produce useable measures of the relative benefits of alternative strategies that in turn will attune policy makers and planners to needs for and benefits of services as well as to their costs.

References and Notes

1. For recent reviews, see: J. Elinson (ed.), Int. J.
    Health Serv. 6(1976); R.L. Berg (ed.), Health Status
    Indexes (Hospital Research and Educational Trust, Chicago,
    1973).

2. We use the term "indicator" to refer to component
    pieces of information that are summarized in a composite
    index.

3. See:World Health Organization, "Statistical Indicators
    for the Planning and Evaluation of Public Health Pro-
    grams," Technical Report Series, No.472 (1971).

4. Ibid., p. 11.

5. Measurement criteria also include empirical standards
    such as validity and reliability, which will not be
    addressed in this paper. For a summary of research on
    this aspect, see: P.W. Haberman, in Poverty and Health:
    A Sociological Analysis, J. Kosa, A. Antonovsky, and
    I. K. Zola (eds.) (Harvard University Press, Cambridge,
    1969), p.343.

6. D.F. Sullivan, "Conceptual Problems in Developing an
    Index of Health," National Center for Health Statistics,
    Series 2, No. 17 (1966).

7. J.W. Bush, M.M. Chen, and D.L. Patrick, "Social Indica-
    tors for Health Based on Function Status and Prognosis,"
    processed, n.d.

8. C.L. Chiang, "An Index of Health: Mathematical Models,"
    National Center for Health Statistics, Series 2, No. 5
    (1965).

9. D.F. Sullivan, "A Single Index of Mortality and Morbid-
    ity," HSMHA Health Reports 86,347 (1971).

10. M.K. Chen, in R.L. Berg, op. cit., p.28.

11. D.S. Levine and D.E. Yett, in R.L. Berg, op. cit., p.13.

12. See, for instance, D.C. Holloway, in R.L. Berg, op. cit.,
    p.89.

13. M.K. Chen, Int. J. Epidemiol. 4,87 (1975).

14. J.W. Bush, et al., in R.L. Berg, op. cit., p.172;
     S. Fanshel and J.W. Bush, Oper. Res. 18,1021 (1970);
     D.L. Patrick, et al., J. Health Soc. Beh. 14,6 (1973).

15. M. Bergner, et al., Int. J. Health Serv. 6,393 (1976).

16. T.W. Bice, Int. J. Health Serv. 6,509 (1976).

9

Health Status Indicators as Tools for Health Planning

Marilyn Bergner

The mandated incorporation of a measured assessment of
need and effectiveness into the planning and policy making
of local and national government occurred for the first time
in the United States with the passage of Public Law 93-641,
the National Health Planning and Resource Development Act.
In establishing a national system for health planning and
regulation, Public Law 93-641 requires that Health Systems
Agencies measure the health status of the populations for
which they are responsible, implying that they plan programs
and assess their effectiveness with reference to that
measure. An assessment such as this is rarely part of the
political process.

During the past ten to twenty years, as the cost of
medical care increased, technological advances became more
wisdespread, and the causal relationship between social
intervention programs and individual or societal improvement
appeared more tenuous, policy-makers encouraged social scientists to devote increasing effort to measuring the effect of
health care on health. These efforts were presumed to lead
to the development of models of the health care system that
would reliably relate programs to outputs and costs and
would inform policy decisions in the area of resource allocation. Though such models have yet to be developed, progress and interest in the measurement of the output, health
staus, seemed sufficiently advanced to incorporate measurement of that output in new planning legislation.

The Needs of Health Planners

Most health planners who are associated with governmental or quasi-governmental agencies and concerned with a relatively broad geographic area, need some way of estimating
health status for defined population groups or geographic
areas. From these estimates they may then discern

differences in health status levels. They also need a way
to estimate the need for health services in general and then
to determine whether specific services are more or less
needed than others. Of course, the latter requires data
beyond that provided by the global estimation of health
status. Such information as the difference in health status
between social groups, ethnic groups, groups treated by different medical care programs, different age groups, different
sex groups are all necessary in order to develop sophisticated health plans (1).

    For the health planner, the problems and questions
associated with the use of health status measures may seem
far greater than the solutions they promise. Whereas PL 93-
641 regulations specify in some detail the goals and standards that are to be met by health planning agencies, the
health status indicators to be used are noticeably lacking.
In a few cases such as infant mortality or communicable
disease mortality, the indicator is obvious; in others
such as functional capacity of the chronically disabled the
indicator is glaringly absent.

    Three broad categories of health indicators have tra-
ditionally been considered appropriate for determining
health levels. They are measures of mortality, measures of
morbidity, and measures of disability or dysfunction. Each
of these categories of measures present different problems
for the planner. In choosing a measure, the planners must
appraise its relevance, availability, and cost to collect,
as well as assess its reliability and validity. Many
planners have wisely chosen to rely on mortality as the
indicator of health status in obtaining a first estimate of
health status levels. Crude mortality rates are uniformly
available and reliable. Often they can be obtained for
relatively small geographic areas. The usefulness of mortality data can be further enhanced by computing age and sex
specific rates. Once disease specificity is added to these
data however, the reliability and validity may drop. The
National Center for Health Statistics has recently looked
at the availability and usefulness of infant mortality and
perinatal mortality as indicators of health status at the
county level. Kleinman, Feldman and Mugge (2) of the
National Center argue, rather convincingly, that infant
mortality is an excellent indicator that has been available
for a long time, and that it may be particularly useful in
determining comparative need for services for both infants
and mothers. However, they caution all planners that for
counties with few births and thus low absolute mortality,
the standard error of the data may be so large as to render
it essentially useless. Thus, though the data is reliable

in the sense of being accurate, it is unreliable in the sense
that data for any single year may be subject to wide variation.

Nonetheless, mortality data could provide planners with
"first cut" estimates of health status. The crude death
rate could be used to rank different geographic areas or
different population subgroups. But it would not suffice
to do program planning. In the simplest model for determining health need in terms of health status, areas with high
crude death rates would be examined further to determine age
specific, sex specific and disease specific mortality rates.
Again, these could be ranked and used to identify areas with
poor health status. But once these are determined, still
further specification is needed in order to develop adequate
and relevant program plans. The planner is then faced with
a choice from among a variety of morbidity statistics, a
group of indices that profess to combine morbidity and mortality into a single measure (3,4,5), and a group of beha-
viorally based function assessment measures that presumably
can provide indications of health status independent of
medical care (6,7,8).

The planner who chooses to look at health status in
terms of morbidity data is faced with incomplete data collection, unreliable determination of morbid states and
questions concerning the relevance of the data. Knowing that
many people suffer from rheumatoid arthritis in one group
and angina in another provides no indication of which should
be remedied, or how, in the likely event that a choice must
be made. What is the potential for "curing" arthritis as
compared to angina? What impact does a particular disease
have on the population and on medical care services? What
are the preferences of the population in question?

Available Health Status Measures

Many health planners are trying to work out ways of
measuring health status that will provide them with information they can use in rational health planning, decision
making, and eventually in improving the health status they
now wish to measure. Planners are aggregating every possible variable related to health status, without regard to
cause and effect, or input or output, so that they can
identify areas of high need. Sometimes they are working
in conjunction with consultant methodologists and statisticians. Rarely is anyone in the academic or scientific
community associated with these attempts. One wonders if
that is the result of a communication gap between those in
government and regulation and those in the academic

community. Or, if it stems from the reluctance of academics
to work on problems that may be complex, difficult to solve,
and that require lengthy time commitments and thus do not
fit the usual reward system of academia (9). Whatever the
cause, the effect is the generation of innumerable indices
of questionable reliability, validity and relevance, that
do not require new data collection, but do require the recom-
bination and recalculation of already collected data that is,
in itself, of questionable reliability and validity. Arbitrary weighting procedures and the use of data that violate
the assumptions of the statistics employed in calculating
the indices, are two readily identifiable sources of bias.
Furthermore, sophisticated statistical consultants often
make use of sophisticated statistical techniques even when
they are technically inappropriate. They understand the
limitations or shortcomings of the statistics generated;
their planning counterparts often do not. Numbers are taken
at face value and complex associations, distributions, or
interactions that are the underpinning of the statistic are
ignored. Principal component analysis and factor analysis
are being used by some planning agencies to combine discrete
data into health indices. Most planners are unable to
decide on or defend the variables that are included, the
method chosen, or why a summary statistic should be calculated at all.

Yet there are a few epidemiologists, psychologists,
economists and health services researchers who have been
working toward the development of health status indicators.
Some of this work has concentrated on the development of
scaled indices of health-related dysfunction. Such indices
have been thought to be especially pertinent for health
planning since they include an estimate of the value that
society places on certain activities or conditions, do not
require that a professional assess the "health" of the
individual, and are readily understandable. They can be
incorporated into cost benefit analyses, into analyses of
health status change, and into complex models of health
system organization and behavior.

The Health Status Index developed by Bush, Patrick and
Chen (6), the Function Status Index of Miles, Rushing and
Reynolds (7), and the Sickness Impact Profile (10) are all
examples of indices aimed at providing planners and policy
makers with information to be applied to resource allocation decisions. They are all based on information gathered
by questionnaire. The questionnaire is structured and
standardized, that is, it contains predetermined items
arranged in a predetermined format. Each item is assigned
a weight or value thus permitting the calculation of an

overall score. Average scores for population subgroups can
be calculated, compared and followed over time. In terms
of mathematical properties, these indices can be incorporated into cost-effectiveness and linear and mathematical
programming models (11).

Differences among these health status indices result
from differences in the scope, detail, sensitivity, and
weighting procedure. The Sickness Impact Profile measures
dysfunction in 12 areas of activity with 136 items; the
Health Status Index measures dysfunction in three areas of
activity describing 30 function states with a minimum of
13 items. Though weighting procedures differ, their aim
is always the same, to provide a consensually arrived at
value for the activity or dysfunction under consideration.
By incorporating such values (as weights) directly into the
health status score, arbitrary decisions about the worth of
one activity, person, or program are minimized.

Each of the indices has been tested for reliability
and validity (7,12,13). Again, techniques and procedures
differ as may some of the underlying assumptions regarding
reliability and validity, but the arguments and data are
readily available to anyone concerned about choosing the
"right" index for a particular situation.

The use of these indices presupposes the resources and
skill necessary to collect data in a survey-like manner from
populations or samples of populations. Self-administered
forms are available but can only be used with subjects able
to complete them independently. When this is not the case --
the very sick or those with language or reading problems
are examples -- then an interviewer must administer the
questionnaire. The specific costs associated with data
collection are highly dependent on the concentration of the
population and availability of the individual subjects.
A "captive" population such as patients in long term care
institutions, would be relatively inexpensive to interview,
or to have complete a self-administered questionnaire. The
time to complete any one of the above mentioned indices
ranges from 10 to 30 minutes.

To further support the use of these indices is a growing body of experience and data that could provide planners
with comparisons that are clearly important in deciding relative need. These data include the levels and profiles of
health status scores for various segments of the population
and for several diagnostic categories, as well as data
that could begin to provide information on the determinants

of health status. For the most part, these data are only
available from the investigator who developed the indices.
But, speaking for those who developed the Sickness Impact
Profile, we are pleased to share our data in order to
encourage others to use the instrument and thus gain more
information on applicability, feasibility and interrela-
tionships.

<u>Reflections on the Limited Use</u>
<u>of Health Status Indices</u>

What is continually surprising is that the functionally
based health status indices have not been considered for
inclusion in the as yet undefined data set to be used by
planners and policy makers to determine and support program
and policy decisions. Though I could cite several examples
of program evaluation in which a health status index is
being or was used, I personally know of only one instance in
which one of the aforementioned health status indicators is
being used for planning. Two rural communities in Vermont
have allocated funds to determine long term care needs as
part of their planning process. The consultant firm they
hired to help them coincidentally had a research-minded
staff member who reviewed the literature and found the Sickness Impact Profile. He contacted the SIP staff, pilot
tested the instrument himself, and was quickly convinced
that this already tested and validated instrument would suit
his needs and would enhance the credibility of any results
he obtained. Two aspects of this particular application
stand out: first, that there was money allocated to collect
new data and, second, that the person designated to help in
the collection of that data had a research orientation. It
will be extremely interesting to find out how useful the
data collected in those two Vermont counties will be in
developing their long term care plans. If it is, it will
provide an extremely strong argument for the provision of
adequate funds and personnel to permit the utilization of
newly developed health indicator measures.

It is apparent that lack of funds is one of the major
impediments to use of new measures. I suppose that the
limitation placed on expenditures for new data collection
is supported by past experience. Data generated from one-
time surveys are often not relevant to the issues under
investigation, and data collection is costly both in time
and money. But with the development of new health status
measures on the one hand, and a mandate for planners to use
indicators of health status on the other, it seems inconsis-
tent to proscribe data collection. It is worth noting that
the development of the indicators is taking place with the

support of one federal agency and their use is being suggested by another. Neither has taken the initiative to see how
the two can fit together. In some areas, it may be less
costly and more productive to collect new data than to
develop new techniques for handling old data. In many cases
it could be argued that data collection on small, well-
designated samples would substantially further the planning
process and would permit further refinement and development
of health status indicators and of health planning.

In any case, it does seem that there are a few health
status indices that are ready for use by health planners.
Their value in some instances seems apparent, in others only
presumed. Their use at this point would inform both planners and researchers.

Such efforts could have the added benefit of bringing
these two groups together and generating collaborative efforts in this area as well as others. Perhaps experience
with such tools and such collaboration will permit evaluation
of the impact of information on the eternally political
process of public agency planning and management.

References and Notes

1. Data on medical and health care facilities, utilization, social conditions, etc., are also necessary in order to assess service needs, but for simplicity they are ignored in this paper.

2. J.C. Kleinman, J.J. Feldman, R.H. Mugge, Public Health Reports 91,423 (1976).

3. C.L. Chiang, "An Index of Health: Mathematical Models," National Center for Health Statistics, Series 2, No. 5 (1965).

4. M.K. Chen, Inquiry 13,228 (1976).

5. D.F. Sullivan, HSMHA Health Reports 86,347 (1971).

6. D.L. Patrick, J.W. Bush, M.M. Chen, Journal of Health and Social Behavior 14,6 (1973).

7. W.J. Reynolds, W.A. Rushing, D.L. Miles, Journal of Health and Social Behavior 15,271 (1974).

8. B.S. Gilson, J.S. Gilson, M. Bergner, R.A. Bobbitt, S. Kressel, W.E. Pollard, M. Vesselago, American Journal of Public Health 65,1304 (1975).

9. H. Freeman and C.C. Sherwood, in Program Evaluation in the Health Fields, H.C. Schulberg, A. Sheldon, F. Baker, Eds. (Behavioral Publications, New York, 1969), pp. 73-91.

10. M. Bergner and R.A. Bobbitt, with S. Kressel, W.E. Pollard, B.S. Gilson, J.R. Morris, International Journal of Health Services 6,393 (1976).

11. J.W. Bush, S. Fanshel, M.M. Chen, Journal of Socio-Economic Planning Sciences 6,49 (1972).

12. R.M. Kaplan, J.W. Bush, C.C. Berry, "Health Status: Validity of an Index of Well-Being." (Paper presented at the 1976 annual meeting of the American Association for the Advancement of Science, Boston, Mass.)

13. M. Bergner, R.A. Bobbitt, W.E. Pollard, D.P. Martin, B.S. Gilson, Medical Care 14,57 (1976).

Index

Activities of Daily Living
(ADL), 49, 73
acute non-lethal diseases
and health status meas-
ures, 67
aging, chronic degenerative
diseases of, 68
Annual Implementation Plan,
7, 115
Applied Statistics Training
Institute (ASTI), 35

British National Health
Service, 57, 62
Bureau of Community Health
Services, 34
Bureau of Health Planning
and Resource Develop-
ment (BHPRD), 35

Capital Expenditures Review
program, 9
catastrophic insurance, 59,
60
Certificate of Need
laws, 8
program, 8
Chen, Martin K., 117, 119,
120
Chiang, C.L., 117
Conference on Health Status
Indicators, 1976, 76
Cooperative Health Statistics System (CHSS), 7,
27, 33, 37, 48
cost-benefit, 115
cost containment, 2, 29
universal health

universal health insur-
ance, 59
Cuba, health service, 57
current functioning, 84, 86,
88

decayed teeth ratio, 105
dental caries, 97-98
disability and dysfunction,
68, 72, 126, 128, 129
disciplinary research health
status indicators, 71
DMF index (Decayed, Missing,
and Filled teeth), 98,
105

emotional-behavioral con-
trol, 90, 91
epidemiologic studies, use
of oral status indexes
in, 96, 97
epidemiology
analytic, 78
descriptive, 77
epidemiology of health, 77

facilities, distribution of,
57
factor analysis, 119
family planning, 34
Federal Employees Health
Benefits Program, 59
Forward Plan for Health, FY
1978-82, 62
functional status indexes,
120, 128

goals, 1, 36, 61, 62